# DON NORI

### *the* Prayer
# GOD
# LOVES
### *to* Answer

DESTINY IMAGE® PUBLISHERS, INC.
P.O. Box 310, Shippensburg, PA 17257-0310

*"Speaking to the Purposes of God for This Generation and for the Generations to Come."*

This book and all other Destiny Image, Revival Press, Mercy Place, Fresh Bread, Destiny Image Fiction, and Treasure House books are available at Christian bookstores and distributors worldwide.

For a U.S. bookstore nearest you, call **1-800-722-6774.**

For more information on foreign distributors, call **717-532-3040.**

Or reach us on the Internet: **www.destinyimage.com.**

ISBN 10: 0-7684-2376-7
ISBN 13: 978-0-7684-2376-1

*For Worldwide Distribution, Printed in the U.S.A.*

1 2 3 4 5 6 7 8 9 10 11 / 09 08 07 06

# ENDORSEMENTS

———⟨☉⟩———

There is a prayer that God will answer every time you pray it. In this book, Don Nori gives a clear biblical basis for you to know that this prayer will be answered by God. His touching illustrations will open your mind to truth that will set you free—in Jesus!

Dr. Billy Joe Daugherty
Pastor, Victory Christian Center
Tulsa, Oklahoma

Too many Christians miss the purposes of God in our lives because we are too busy building our own lives and furthering our own agenda's rather than doing what is on the heart of the

Lord. In his book, *The Prayer God Loves to Answer,* Don Nori reveals how this revelation from God changed his life.

Don is a man who has a depth and a wealth within him to speak and write to the Body of Christ, as well as to those who are willing to give their whole being in unconditional surrender to the Spirit. Following the Spirit of the Lord is a deep expression of worship, a walk of obedience, and demands a willingness to pay whatever price is required so that God's Kingdom and plans will be established on the earth.

He shows us how—through prayer and saying "yes"— God releases His power from Heaven within us and around us. Prayer and saying "yes" is the very essence of a firm foundation for a lifestyle of experiencing God's presence.

Suzanne Hinn

# CONTENTS

# INTRODUCTION

If you have all the answers, this book is not for you.

This book is not for the theologian. It is not for the intellectual. It is certainly not for the religious. It is for the hungry, the desperate, the needy, the simple—those who know that without the Lord there is no fulfillment, no future, no hope, no joy, and no true love.

Jesus is alive, active, concerned, loving, engaged, and determined to answer your prayers. He wants you to learn to pray according to His will. He will always answer your prayers when you pray according to His will. (See First John 5:14-15.)

This wonderful knowledge will enable you to live above the fray, in complete confidence, rest, and trust that you are safe in the palm of God's mighty hand.

Too often people approach prayer with an attitude that says, "Lord, do it my way, not Your way." They think God can be convinced to do things according to their desires instead of according to the wonderful dream that He alone has dreamed for them.

Many other people are looking for just the right prayer formula, a plan to put in place that will ensure that their prayers will be answered.

But this book soothes neither the fleshy desires of man nor his intellectual logic. Rather, it shows you how to pray the Jesus way, by simply saying "yes" to God. You see, just as our Lord responded to His Father with "yes" as a matter of habit, you, too, can learn to trust Him with that same response in your everyday life.

This kind of praying releases great power within you and through you. It affirms and confirms the word that came to Zechariah so many years ago: *"This is the word of the Lord... 'Not by might nor by power, but by My Spirit,' says the Lord of hosts"* (Zech. 4:6).

*"Have I not commanded you? Be strong and of good courage; do not be afraid, nor be dismayed, for the Lord your God is with you wherever you go"* (Joshua 1:9).

# CHAPTER ONE

# It All Began With "Yes"

Sweat streamed down my face in the sweltering heat of an unusually hot August afternoon in 1982. Sultry summer days make it hard to sell anything, but the house payment came every month regardless of the weather, so I decided to go to Carlisle, Pennsylvania, where the best possibility to make a sale within 50 miles would be found.

I got in my car and headed north on Interstate 81 from Shippensburg, just 20 miles south of Carlisle. My wife, Cathy, was expecting our fourth son at the time. I was pastoring and working two jobs to make ends meet. But I am not complaining about this, because we truly were a happy family; we were blessed and cared for by the Lord in every way.

We didn't have the things that the world considers to be signs of success, but we had Him, each other, and a promise that only He could keep.

*"Success is one right choice after another,"* the Lord had said to me. *"Just keep making the choices in front of you. Success is no accident. A string of right choices will find you succeeding and flourishing in Me."*

The tale of Destiny Image Publishers began on that same summer day. It didn't start with any corporate funding. It wasn't founded by a successful businessman with a foolproof business plan and millions of dollars in venture capital. It was started by a man who heard from the Lord and responded with a definite "yes." That man was me.

## *"No One Cares About My Heart"*

During this time, I was the co-pastor of a vibrant, growing church in south-central Pennsylvania. I also worked in the advertising and sales department of a local newspaper. On this particular August day in 1982, I was on my way to meet a client.

While driving to my destination, the Presence of the Lord filled my car. It was awesome and intense. The Lord's Presence was so great, and I was so astounded by it, that He immediately had my full attention! In fact, the burden of the Lord was so heavy that I had to pull my car off the highway.

The next four hours were filled with the most vibrant manifestations of God's Presence that I had ever felt. Almost as if I were watching projected slides, the Lord began to reveal visions of a publishing ministry to me. A publishing ministry!

The heavens opened to me as I sat in my car. A spirit of praise welled up from deep within me, and it was magnificent, for it seemed as if I was actually joining with the heavenly choirs in singing glory to the Lord Most High. I could sense that the heavens were alive with the joy of the Lord and with an eager anticipation of fellowship and worship that flowed into my car and spilled all over me.

During this special time of glory, God spoke to me. He said, *"I have much to say to this generation, but nobody cares. Nobody seems to know that I have much to say."* His voice was filled with an obvious, unspeakable pain as He continued, *"No one cares about My heart. No one cares about My heart."*

As the Lord spoke, I saw another vision. He was in a great room that buzzed with a tremendous flurry of activity. Although I had never been to a trade show of any kind at that point in my life, I knew that in the spirit I was seeing a Christian trade show.

Buyers were scurrying all over the floor. Sellers were hawking their wares loudly. Everyone was too busy to notice that the Lord and I were walking among them.

*"Look at them,"* the Lord said. *"They are all so busy. They all think they are doing My work, building My kingdom, but none of them cares about My heart. None cares about My purposes. No one wants to know what I am doing in the land."*

The Lord paused, as if to let His words sink into my heart; then He continued, *"They are building their own kingdoms, securing their own place in the market. None cares about My heart."*

Tears streamed down my cheeks as I looked to the Lord and cried, "I care about Your heart! I care about what You have to say! You know that I treasure Your words. You know that I melt at the sound of Your voice!"

There was no answer. It was as if the Lord hadn't heard my cry. The vision of the convention floor began to fade, as the images of people hurrying to and fro gradually disappeared like smoke blown by the wind.

## *"I Am Looking for a Prophet"*

However, a new vision replaced the one that was fading away. This time, I found myself looking into a small, cluttered room. I saw an editor sitting at a desk in the center of that room. His sleeves were rolled up to his elbows and he wore a visor on his brow to shield his eyes from the glare of the fluorescent lighting. The editor was busily working on a manuscript, changing words, correcting spelling errors, and muttering quietly.

Slowly, the door to the editor's office swung open, and a man who was wearing a long, flowing robe walked in. This man was carrying a very large stack of paper. Immediately, I knew he was a prophet. Quietly and respectfully, the prophet walked slowly toward the editor's desk. His sandals flapped softly with every step he took.

Without a word, the prophet placed his manuscript in front of the editor, bowing low as he backed away from the desk. Then he stood nervously, pulling at his long beard, as the editor put aside what he was doing and reached for the prophet's book. Without once looking at or addressing the prophet, the editor went to work on the pages of the prophet's book.

Mumbling to himself, the editor began to scratch out large portions of the text with his pen, and he said, "No one wants to hear this!" Occasionally, he even crumpled up entire sheets and threw them away, saying, "You can't say that and get away with it!"

The prophet stood silently as the editor worked. The editor paused. He took a deep breath, removed his glasses, and looked at the prophet. "Don't you get it?" he asked. "You have to tell the people what they want to hear. You only make it look a bit radical, but in the last analysis, you have to then deliver what people want to hear, if you are going to sell books." He then shook his head in frustration and went back to work.

The prophet never responded. He simply lowered his head submissively and silently cringed as the editor dismantled the message God had given to him.

In my heart I knew that the prophet was willing to do anything to get his work published, even if it meant compromising the message. The voice of the Lord rang with indignation as He spoke these words to me: *It is an abomination for My prophets to submit their words to mere mortal men.* As He uttered the last three words, I could sense that their taste in His mouth was very bitter to Him.

He then spoke to my heart once more, *"I am looking for a prophet to publish the prophets."*

In the heat of that early afternoon, as I sat in my car along Interstate 81, I found myself crying out to the Lord: "I care about what You have to say!" Without quite knowing the full import of what He had been saying, I said, "I'll do it! I'll publish the prophets! I care about Your heart! I'll do it!"

To be truthful, I did not realize who or what I was at that point. When the Lord said He was looking for a prophet, I offered to Him that I would find one! But it did not take long for me to understand that God was referring to *me*.

But once again, without response, like smoke being blown by the wind, the vision faded. The sounds of angelic choirs, the heavenly anticipation, and the overflowing joy of the Lord were gone, leaving me alone in my car. All was quiet, except for the dull hum of cars and trucks speeding by on the highway.

I was alone. For a moment, I simply sat in awe at what had just happened, but the abrupt end of the visions troubled me. "Did I say something wrong?" Silence. "Did I say something out of order?" Silence again.

## *"Guard My Word as Silver and Your Integrity as Gold"*

I continued to sit there, pondering my next move. Had it all been a dream? Was it a hallucination? Perhaps it had merely been the product of my overactive imagination. All of these thoughts were bombarding me when, all of a sudden, the heavens opened to me once again!

The glory of ageless wonder and magnificence enveloped me, and a music that went beyond being beautiful once again flowed into my spirit. God then spoke to me: *"If you will guard My Word as silver, and your integrity as gold, I will cause you to publish My prophets."* His deep, resonant voice was speaking to my heart. He continued, *"I will cause you to be to this generation what I intended another to be before you."* My only response to Him was, "Yes, Lord. Whatever You want, I will do it."

As quickly as it had come, the Presence of the Lord lifted. Again, I felt alone in the silence. So, after a time, I eased the car back onto the highway and drove slowly homeward. I knew I had a challenge to face with regard to this burden God had placed deep within my heart. I had to let Cathy know about it, and I wondered how she would respond.

After all, Cathy was pregnant with our fourth son. It was already almost impossible for us to pay our monthly bills. Cathy had worked at a local elementary school, but now with "number four" on the way, it would not make sense for her to work outside the home. God knows it is hard enough to keep four boys and a house in order. Besides, few really understand the power of a loving mom in preparing sons for adulthood.

Now I was about to tell her I wanted to start a publishing company that would publish the prophets and change the world! Uh, of course, I would need to do this full-time. I knew God would have to prepare her heart if this was going to happen.

When I got home, I shared what had taken place with her. She sat in stunned silence as I said, "I think I need to do this." Then I waited for her response of either approval or refusal.

It was now my turn to be stunned, for Cathy told me, "This is our purpose, Don. This is what God has laid upon our hearts for us to do." God had been speaking to her that we were about to do something that would take us in a completely new direction. She had been waiting for me to find out what it was.

So Cathy and I, with our minds full of many questions and our hearts at rest in the Lord, joined together and said "yes" to God. Then we proceeded to discuss the days and months that were ahead of us and the challenges we might face.

## The Name of Our Dream

For several days I felt the Presence of the Lord resting heavily upon me, as God continued to reveal His vision for our lives—the dream He had dreamed for us. Whispers of things that lay many years ahead echoed in my mind. Every time the Lord touched my heart, I repeated, "Yes, Lord. I'll do it. Whatever You want of me, I'll do it."

But we still had a family we were responsible for, so I had to stay focused on earning a living as well. Therefore, I continued to line up sales clients. Although I had two degrees, one in education and another in environmental studies, I knew very little about publishing. I spent my time selling print, printing equipment, and other items related to printing and publishing, as I waited for the Lord's direction.

As it turns out, the contracts I signed as a free commercial printing agent ended up providing the income we needed for several years to come!

As the last day of my regular job approached, I asked the Lord what name I should give to the company He was leading me to start. Almost immediately the voice of the Lord spoke strongly to me, and He said, *"'Destiny Image,' because you are destined to be conformed to My image."*

The new company was born on January 1, 1983. I purchased a small wooden desk from a local auction house and got a black rotary phone to use for the business, which was situated in our living room—the headquarters of a company that would eventually become one of the largest and most respected Full Gospel publishing companies in the Christian world. This came about because of God's mercy and because two people, desperate to do His will, said "Yes."

## *Dreams Are Born Like Infants*

Dreams are born in much the same way as babies are born. Infants arrive on the scene with joy, fanfare, excitement, and wonder. However, the real truth is that a newborn is simply a newborn. He messes his pants and may often stay up all night crying.

A baby consumes vast quantities of valuable resources, such as time, money, and emotional strength, as well. Yet this does not take away from the fact that he is awesome; for in him resides the hope of the future.

The baby becomes the object of lavish affection, as he or she is displayed at family gatherings and church functions with great pride and adoration. Nonetheless, the newborn does require a lot of assistance—which translates to *work* for the parents! He or she is often demanding and seemingly unthankful, and he or she is cute and cuddly as well as frustrating.

The bottom line in all of this is that the infant is yours; and, as his or her parent, you know the child will grow to be the pride and joy that you dream for him or her to be and to become.

God's dream for you is the same. It often comes with the same kind of excitement that you feel in anticipation of the birth of a child, and the same kind of joy that you feel when the child is born. As the dream grows, it becomes a full-time responsibility. You spend your time trying to nurse it to its fullness.

Sometimes it requires so much work that you wonder if it was God who called you to such a big task. But the fruit of obedience can never be denied, and the joy of being in the center of God's will always brings a peace and strength that nothing in this world could ever match.

When Cathy and I said "yes" to Jesus in the budding days of Destiny Image, the cycle was the same. Those first years we spent working out of our living room, as a mom-and-pop business, brought an abundance of trials, uncertainties, and fears, but God always proved Himself faithful to us. Our resolve, nonetheless, was tested time and time again.

Ultimately, the vision of Destiny Image was burned so powerfully and deeply into our hearts that we knew we would never again ask the Lord, "Are You sure we heard You correctly? Are You sure we're the right people for this?"

As I write this some 23 years later, Cathy and I and the staff of Destiny Image still have an ever-growing sense of God's sovereign hand moving in all that we do. From our obscure, tiny beginning, God has raised up a company of people who share the vision of Destiny Image and who, through their faith in the Lord, are *truly* changing the world.

*We can never forget that it all began with a simple, three-letter word: "Yes!"*

*"...His compassions fail not. They are new every morning; great is Your faithfulness. 'The Lord is my portion,' says my soul. 'Therefore I hope in Him!' The Lord is good to those who wait for Him, to the soul who seeks Him"* (**Lamentations 3:22-25**).

Jesus said, *"Ask, and it will be given to you; seek, and you will find; knock, and it will be opened to you"* (Matthew 7:7).

# CHAPTER TWO

# God's "Skeleton Key" Prayer

My grandpap was the person who introduced me to the skeleton key. It happened in a way that was both scary and funny, but I learned something important that day. As I think about it now, it seems like something that took place a million years ago.

I was only six years old, and I was with my grandpap when he discovered that he was locked out of his garage just down the hill from his house. He told me to run up to the house and ask Grandma for the skeleton key hanging in the kitchen closet.

Now I had never heard of a skeleton key before, and the mere mention of the word "skeleton" scared me to death!

I checked to see if I had heard him right. "What do you want me to get?"

"I want to open the garage door, but I left the keys in the car. Grandma has a skeleton key hanging in the kitchen closet," said Grandpap.

Well, I felt a curl of fear ripple up my back as I walked toward the house. I really had no idea what I would be getting from Grandma, but the mere thought of it frightened me. By the time I reached the kitchen door, I had worked myself into quite a "fit," and I was sobbing from fear.

Grandma heard me crying and turned from the sink to see me walk through the screen door with my head hanging low.

"What is wrong with you, Boy?" she asked.

"Grandpap says there is a skeleton hanging in the kitchen closet. He is going to make me carry it down to the garage for him," I said.

Through my tear-filled eyes, I had hoped to see some look of pity on Grandma's face, but she just smiled and gave me the key.

To this day I am still haunted by the memory of the time when I thought Grandpap wanted me to get a skeleton out of the kitchen closet!

## A Skeleton Key Will Open Anything

Skeleton keys are no longer as commonplace as they used to be, and those that do exist don't look like the old ones did. However, the principle of the skeleton key remains the same. It is a key that will open almost any door.

Skeleton keys are amazing. Whoever invented them deserves more recognition than he has received. No matter what door in a house is locked, a skeleton key will open it, allowing you to enter. It is certainly an amazing invention.

But God has a "skeleton key" too, and it works every time. In fact, His "skeleton key" never fails.

For years I searched for a key that would open Heaven every time I prayed. I wanted to know that God would both hear my prayer and respond to my heart when I talked to Him.

I began to hunt for a prayer that He would absolutely love—a prayer that would give me the peace of heart and mind that comes from knowing He is at work in response to what I ask Him to do.

After years of searching, it came to me one day that all I need to do is to ask God to do what He already wants to do! This is the only thing that assures me He will answer my prayers.

## One Little Word

What I've just described is a very simple way to pray. That's probably why I had overlooked it for so many years.

God's "skeleton key prayer" is simply saying "yes" to Him. Who would have ever imagined that such a simple, three-letter word would unlock the passion and power within God's heart? Such a concept had never occurred to me.

I have discovered, however, that it is the one key that always works. It never fails to release the delight and favor of God.

It works simply because it is the Father's joy for us to agree with Him. He has a plan for *each of us*—a plan that He fully intends to bring to pass in our lives. I just love it, and that is why I'm sharing it with you.

## "Thy Kingdom Come; Thy Will Be Done"

God wants to have a relationship with His children. In fact, this is why He created us. His approach to this dynamic relationship is very simple, but many of us work too hard at it, and we end up complicating it way beyond our own ability to even understand it!

When Jesus taught us to pray, He let us in on this little "skeleton key" secret. He prayed, *"Your kingdom come. Your will be done on earth as it is in heaven"* (Matt. 6:10).

This tells us something very simple. God wants His plan for us to be accomplished on our planet, just as His will is being done in Heaven. Later, He goes on to tell us something very remarkable about His own willingness to do what His Father wants Him to do.

Jesus said, *"I can of Myself do nothing. As I hear, I judge; and My judgment is righteous, because I do not seek My own will but the will of the Father who sent Me"* (John 5:30).

Jesus was and still is totally committed to His Father's plan. He knew that the full purpose for His life as well as for all life on this planet is found in doing what God wanted Him to do. In short, He learned to say "yes" to His Father.

Jesus said, *"When you lift up the Son of Man, then you will know that I am He, and that I do nothing of Myself; but as My Father taught Me, I speak these things"* (John 8:28).

Jesus moved, walked, talked, and prayed in accord with His Father's will. He taught us to pray in agreement with the Father as well. The prayer He taught His disciples still works today, as it did when Jesus walked on earth.

In fact, I have discovered that this approach to prayer always works, no matter what the attitude of my heart and mind or the circumstances of my life may be. God responds to me without regard to my momentary mood swings or the doctrines of my church. He responds to me according to the counsel of His will and without regard to how what I have been taught might conflict with His purposes for me. His plan has the preeminence in my life, and as long as I agree with Him, nothing that the world, the religious system, or the enemy can do will stop it. And He will do the same for you!

You see, God has a one-track mind. He wants His dream for humanity, and for you, His child, to be fulfilled. He will bring it to pass as you simply accept and trust the desires of *His* heart.

The power of Heaven is released when we agree with His purposes and dreams for us. That's why I call this approach God's "skeleton key prayer." It works every time, no matter what may be happening to you emotionally or spiritually.

Does this sound like it's too good to be true? Really, it's too true to be ignored. It makes perfect sense when you look at things from the perspective of God's love and desire for you, His child.

He wants always to give good gifts to you. (See James 1:17.) That's why Jesus has presented you with a style of praying that transcends all hindrances—the things that block you from reaching God and block Him from reaching you.

## Agreeing With God

What does the "skeleton key prayer" do? It asks God to do His perfect will in your life. By praying "yes," you are agreeing with Him and His Word, even when you do not understand what His Word may mean. He understands His own Word, and that is all that is necessary!

When I can trust Him to do something that I do not understand, I am no longer polluting the spiritual atmosphere with my own fleshy desires. I am setting my mind and my heart to trust Him, even in what I do not understand. God responds to our words. When we pray according to our own fleshy desires or our opinions or even earthy reason, we pollute the spirit with things that should not have the right to speak before God.

Have you ever wondered what to pray and how to pray it? I think most of us have been fearful that we might approach and engage in prayer in the wrong way or say the wrong things. Has this kind of confusion about prayer ever prevented you from asking for God's help when you wanted and needed it the most?

If so, you are not alone.

I have spoken in churches around the world. I have talked to countless people who have been going through the most challenging circumstances imaginable.

One thing I've learned about people the world over is that most want to pray or they want to have someone pray for them during troubled times. Most people are desperate to pray, but they just don't know how.

God's "skeleton key prayer" cuts through all the misinformation we have received through the years. It transcends doctrines and dogmas about prayer. It opens every door that God wants open in our lives. If the door does not open with this prayer, He does not want it open at the time you are praying for it to open.

If you have never received teaching about prayer, agreeing with God will give you a "head start" in seeing Him begin to work in your life.

Though many people have been schooled in churches about prayer, they never really experience the power and results that come from agreeing with God in a genuine relationship with Him, a relationship that comes from trusting Him, even if you do not know what He wants.

When you learn to say "yes" to your heavenly Father, a sense of brokenness begins to work within you. You are submitting your will to His, your desires to His desires, your plan for His dream. It will open your heart to Him. This enables you to hear Him say things to you that you never heard before and think things you never thought before. Then you will most certainly do things you have never done before. It completely changes your perspective.

God wants to bring us to Himself so He can accomplish His will in our lives, but this requires our commitment to Him and our willingness to agree with Him.

## Don't Be Afraid of Your Emotions

Several things may hinder our prayers and cause us not to experience God's answers.

The emotions resulting from fear, guilt, depression, and a poor self-image always sap our strength, and they cause us to lose our hope in God. These feelings may lead us to think that God doesn't even care about us.

If you think He doesn't really care, you will doubt that He has any good plans for your life. When you are emotionally distraught, it is difficult to know what you should pray for or how you should pray.

Don't be afraid of your emotions; God created them for specific purposes. As time goes on, you will begin to hear His voice and understand His Spirit who communicates to your heart in a variety of ways.

When you are certain that you have heard God tell His will to you, then you will automatically begin to pray specifically as He has shown. The important thing, though, is to be sure it was His voice. In reality, most people do not have trouble hearing His voice; they have trouble obeying His voice. This rebellion against His voice often results in self-made confusion. For it is not that we do not hear His voice, rather it is that we do not want to hear what He is saying. In this event, we often say that we are not sure about His plan or that we are too confused to hear Him. Godly counsel from people we know and love is best at this point. Consult with those whom you are sure have your best interest at heart with no hidden agenda that would benefit themselves—that is the safest course.

As Jesus heard the Father, He judged. As He heard the Father, He obeyed according to what He knew He had heard. He did not allow human emotions to overrule His knowledge of God's will.

Be careful about this, for it is very easy to let our emotions gain control of us and rule over our desires, and it is extremely easy to allow our hidden desires—some of which may stem from past hurts, sorrows, and losses—to steer our hearts in a way that is contrary to God's will for us. In so doing we are likely to respond to our self-interests and the pains of the past rather than to the Holy Spirit and the words He speaks to us.

It is essential for us to judge as Jesus did before we take action regarding what we hear.

*"For the word of God is living and powerful, and sharper than any two-edged sword, piercing even to the division of soul and spirit, and of joints and marrow, and is a discerner of the thoughts and intents of the heart"* **(Hebrews 4:12).**

## *The Power of Our Emotions*

In the past, many of us have been taught not to trust our emotions. Some of us have been led to believe that emotions are bad, and they will always lead us astray. This is errant teaching, and it has even led some to believe that God is void of any emotions.

Some have taught that God's Presence is a strictly subjective thing, and a sense of His nearness is just a matter of opinion. What a tragedy this is, for it causes God's people to miss the very excitement and joy that His love for us always engenders.

Certainly emotions should not be ignored, for we do need to understand them and what they are saying to us. They are not enemies of our souls. The truth is that they can serve to greatly enhance our relationship with God.

When considering emotions, it's important to remember that we were created in the image and likeness of God. He loves us with an everlasting love. Who would ever want to be in a loveless marriage or raise children in a vacuum that is devoid of love, joy, and compassion?

Instead of fearing our emotions, let's embrace them so we will learn to discern and understand them in the light of faith. As we mature in faith, our discernment will serve to show us the difference between human emotions and God's will. This is a vital part of growing to full maturity in Jesus Christ.

There are many things that God wants to say to us and do through us. He is looking for people who are more interested in building His Kingdom than they are in building their own kingdoms.

*Jesus said, "But seek first the kingdom of God and His righteousness, and all these things shall be added to you"* **(Matthews 6:33).**

## Come as You Are. . .or Feel!!

Years ago, on a beautiful autumn afternoon, I was burning brush and leaves just beyond the fence row behind our property. My wife, Cathy, had just put our five sons down for a nap. All was well, or so I thought.

It was such a peaceful afternoon. I let the fire burn down to embers, then I left to go into the house to drink some fresh lemonade Cathy had made for us.

Unbeknown to us, our fourth son, Joel, who was only four, got up from his nap and ventured out, barefooted, into our back-yard. Like most children, he always seemed to be filled with curiosity, and this time was no exception, for he walked through the gate and straight into the embers of the fire!

After only a few steps onto those burning coals, Joel knew he was in big trouble. He realized he needed help, and he needed it fast! He headed back to the house, but the more he walked on his scorched feet, the more they hurt. The more they hurt, the more he ran. The more he ran, well, you understand.

Our little boy was in trouble, and he had a message and a request for help to deliver to us.

How do you suppose he approached "the thrones of grace" who were sitting in the kitchen sipping lemonade?

I can assure you that he did not approach us with a formal entreaty such as: "Mother, Father, greetings! Something terrible has happened to me just now. I know that I have not been the shining example of 'sonship' this morning. I know that I caused you grief when I poured syrup into my brother's shoes. Oh, you didn't know it was me who did that? Well, yes, it was me, and I'm sorry. Could you find it in your heart to forgive me? I am currently in dire straits, and I need to clear my heart before I can ask for your help...."

No, that was not the way he approached us. Not in a million lifetimes! It was more like this: Joel came *wailing* through the yard, the sound of his "near death" experience reaching our ears long before he got to us. In fact, it took us less than a second to fly through the kitchen door, reach our son, embrace him, and give him comfort.

In less than three minutes Cathy was on her way to the emergency room with Joel, while I stayed with the other children!

Joel didn't have to say anything. He did not have to remind us of his failures or confess his sins to us. He did not have to ask for our favor or try to restore his relationship with us.

You see, he had our love simply because he was our son. He had our favor simply because he was ours! It is the same with God. He loves you. He knows your needs. He wants to be close to you.

God is just waiting for you to come to Him.

*Jesus said, "If you...know how to give good gifts to your children, how much more will your Father who is in heaven give good things to those who ask Him!"* (Matthew 7:11).

## Living Above the Fray

To live in the "yes" of God is to live above the fray, above the flesh, in the Spirit, where Christ is. It is to be seated in the heavenly places with Him. (See Ephesians 1:3.)

This is transcendence of the highest order, for the "yes" of God is a dimension of obedience and trust in the Lord. It is a place of rest, peace, and joy. It is the experience of His Presence every day.

In this realm you will experience His love and power flowing freely to you, in you, and through you. These things don't happen, however, simply because you are "claiming" something or insisting that God must answer you.

You don't experience His love and power because you've been "good." When you learn to live in the "yes" of God, you don't really expect anything but Him, and your concern is to be near to Him, living joyfully in His Presence, as you anticipate the sound of His voice.

George MacDonald wrote, "The purposes of God point to one simple end—that we should be as He is, think the same thoughts, mean the same things, possess the same blessedness." This is the dream He dreams for you.

In the dimension of "yes" you are not concerned with interpretations of the Bible, denominational biases, or theological points of view. Your focus is not on religion or dogma; your focus is on serving God and being a co-laborer with Him.

You know that He will always do His part as you learn to listen for His voice and respond to Him.

Again, George MacDonald makes this quite clear for us. He wrote, "God is here with him [man and woman], upholding, warming, delighting, teaching him—making life a good thing to him. God gives him Himself."

Experiencing God's Presence is the lifestyle purchased for us by Jesus on the cross. Learning to agree with Him and living above the fray of fleshy, everyday life—above the struggles of ordinary men and women who may be more concerned with religious "political correctness" than they are with responding to

God's voice—is the real key to peace with God and the fullness of life in Him.

It is difficult for some to see this, but God does not move according to our doctrines, denominations, and systems. He does not seek permission from church boards, elders, deacons, committees, or bishops. He moves according to His own will in order to accomplish His purposes on the earth.

It is good to know that God is not bound by humanity's religious or secular "tunnel vision." He will change the world through simple folk who will allow Him to change, rearrange, and challenge the fortresses of their shallow thinking, even if that shallowness is disguised as "deep theological wisdom" or scientific intellectualism; these things are just foolishness in His eyes.

As we learn to live above the fray, in the "yes" of God, we will no longer make choices and decisions based upon our five physical senses or our ability to reason. Instead, we will seek the Lord's wisdom, which comes to us through spiritual analysis and understanding, not through the intellect, the emotions, education, or the physical senses.

Living above the fray is abiding in the place of confidence that comes from realizing that God knows the end from the beginning, and He is leading us each step of our way.

By "the fray" I mean anything that is fleshy and clouds the spiritual reality of God's love for us. The fray consists of all those things that keep our thoughts earthbound instead of Jesus-centered. The fray causes us to doubt the dream God has for us and causes us to think less of ourselves, thus forgetting who we are and why we were born.

Training ourselves to think, believe, and trust God above the fray is the beginning of life in the "yes" of God, where the spiritual air is clear, and His voice is easily recognizable.

Living in this realm is knowing God intimately and having His assurance within your heart at all times.

## *You Can Say "Yes" to God*

God is not looking for people who will attempt to serve Him in an advisory capacity. He wants people who will say "yes" to Him. And you can say "yes" to God because you know certain things about Him and His ways.

First, you can say "yes" to Him simply because you know Him and you know He loves you. You can say "yes" to God because you know that you are saved and that you are in a constant state of being forgiven.

Another reason why you can say "yes" to God is that you know you are filled with the Holy Spirit. And you can say "yes" to Him because you know that He hears your prayers and knows what you have need of before you express it to Him.

Finally, you can say "yes" to God because you know He is *for* you, and He has dreamed a dream for you that no one can take away from Him, for He holds it in His heart for you alone.

In light of all these truths, it is time for you to say "yes" to God, remembering that *this* is His "skeleton key prayer" that keeps you in the center of His will and above the fray.

**Jesus said, "…your Father knows the things you have need of before you ask Him"** (Matthew 6:8).

### SCRIPTURE REFERENCES FOR FURTHER STUDY

| | |
|---|---|
| 2 Corinthians 1:20 | Psalm 63:3 |
| Psalm 106:1 | Nehemiah 8:10 |
| 1 John 4:18 | Ephesians 3:20 |
| 1 John 4:6-7 | 2 Corinthians 3:18 |
| Romans 8:38-39 | Psalm 68:19 |
| Romans 5:5 | 1 John 5:14-15 |

The Psalmist writes, *"Because he has set his love upon Me, therefore I will deliver him; I will set him on high, because he has known My name. He shall call upon Me, and I will answer him; I will be with him in trouble; I will deliver him and honor him"* (Psalm 91:14-15).

# CHAPTER THREE

# God Has Dreamed
## a Dream for You

God has dreamed a dream for His people. He has dreamed a dream for you. He has dreamed a dream that no man, no spirit, and no sin can ever cancel. He holds your dream in His heart, waiting for the moment when you will turn to Him and agree with Him. He holds it securely within Him, and He anticipates with great joy your decision to walk with Him.

His Spirit is brooding over His people in order to bring fresh light, revelation, and order to them. His Spirit is brooding over you. When the Spirit of the Lord broods over His people, He delivers a word from the Lord—a word that awaits our response.

Truly, He broods over His people because there is something they need to accomplish, certainly as a body, but also as individuals. He wants to teach us the joy and fulfillment that come from agreeing with Him so that His dream for us can be fulfilled.

Saying "yes" to Jesus every day will change your life, your world, and your perspective on nearly everything. It will give you hope and a sense of true destiny that will come in no other way. When you do so, He will set into motion a series of events and circumstances that will bring your life into perfect harmony with what He has planned for you.

Fleshy and aggressive self-promotion will not be "needed" any longer, for agreeing with God will release the power of Heaven that will give you favor in ways you could never realize on your own.

The minute you surrender your future to God, you are submitting your will to His will, admitting that you were born with divine purpose. You are not on this planet just to wander over the earth aimlessly; you were planted where you are because God, who knew you before you were born, has a plan for your life. (See Jeremiah 1:5.)

**You see, Heaven is our destination, but it is not our destiny. God has an amazing future for you that is fraught with adventure and fulfillment exactly suited to your temperament and gifting. Some see destiny as a point in time, a place, or a career. But destiny is far greater than an event. Destiny is wrapped in God's overall desire to see His people fulfilled, functional, and full of His joy as they respond to Him each day. A "yes" before the throne of God opens doors that no man can open and releases the work of angels to bring about everything that is needed to bring you into all that He has dreamed for you.**

Many of us spend our days complaining, not understanding the mighty hand of God that is so active in our lives. We ask questions like, "But, Lord, why can't I be somewhere else? Why can't I be living somewhere else? Why can't I be doing something different? Why don't I look better? Why don't I have more money to serve You with?"

But, as we ask these questions, we are defying His will for our lives. In effect, we are saying, "I don't like what God has done, where He has put me. Maybe if I complain enough, He will change my circumstances."

May God help us to see and understand the depth of His activity in our lives. He is so intricately involved with our lives that He even knows the number of hairs on our heads, even as they begin to fall out! (See Matthew 10:30.)

Often we forget that God has put us where we are with specific purposes in mind. We are in a school, as it were, and the circumstances of life serve to train us and prepare us for what is to come. We are living in important times, and we must begin to understand that God has put us where we are in preparation for what is yet to come.

If you have the courage to stop complaining about your situation, the courage to accept God's plan, you will begin to perceive His marvelous activity in your life. You will see His hand moving in your daily circumstances, giving you the fortitude and hope to continue to submit your life into His hands.

We often become discouraged because we do not understand His workings and begin to feel so alone. But He is near you, gently loving you, healing you, restoring you, and drawing you to Himself as He leads you into the dream He has dreamed for you.

Meister Eckhart put it well when he said, "For however devoted you are to [God], you may be sure that He is immeasurably more devoted to you."

This is why the Holy Spirit broods over you. He broods over His people, waiting for them to say, "Yes, I accept where I am, who I am, what I am. Yes, I accept the occupation I'm in. Yes, I accept the way I look. I know You have put me right where I am. You have made me exactly what I am, and I know You have a plan for my life in the here-and-now, right where I am. So, Lord, I say 'yes' to You. Do with me what You will. Take me. Mold me. Release Your dream into the center of my life." It will be at least difficult, if not impossible, for God to carry you to the fullness of His dream for you if you cannot accept where you are. This is the beginning; it may not be the end, but it is the beginning, for it is where you are.

Since I have begun to understand this mighty prayer, everything in my life has changed. It used to be that when I woke up in the morning, went to the bathroom, and prepared to shave, I would look in the mirror and think, "Man, you're so ugly and worthless. Nobody will receive from you. God can't use somebody like you. What can you do for the Lord?"

My negative self-image would throw me into a downward spiral at the beginning of each new day.

This meant that I would have to spend several minutes, if not hours, trying to like myself better and trying to gain self-acceptance, instead of spending my time responding to what God had called me to do. It was horrible.

Then one morning I heard God speak to my heart. He said, *"O, My son, I will use you to change the world. You and I are going to get 'em today!"*

I couldn't believe it at first. Religion had taught me that I was always falling short of God's glory, that I could never be "good" enough.

But my heavenly Father had a different message for me that morning—a message that has altered my outlook ever since. Now I wake up most mornings with a new attitude, an attitude that proclaims, "Yes, we're going to get 'em today!"

By learning to do this on a daily basis, I am learning to accept myself as I am and even to love myself. It has meant all the difference in the world to me.

## Don't Be Like a Mule or a Horse

The Psalmist wrote, *"I will instruct you and teach you in the way you should go; I will guide you with My eye. Do not be like the horse or like the mule, which have no understanding, which must be harnessed with bit and bridle, else they will not come near you"* (Ps. 32:8-9).

A bit in the mouth of a horse or mule can cause much pain for them because it fits right across their mouths and pushes against the backs of their mouths. In order to make the animal turn, you pull on the reins, and this pinches the animal's mouth, causing a lot of pain.

The horse or mule doesn't turn because it wants to obey or please its master; it turns because it knows that turning will relieve the pain.

Bystanders may watch and say, "My, what an obedient horse that is!" They think they're seeing obedience in action, but what they're really seeing is pain-avoidance. When the rider wants to turn right, he or she pulls hard on the reins, and the horse turns to the right in order to get rid of the pain in its mouth. It soon understands that unless it turns as directed, the pain will be unbearable.

This is not what God has called us to: a life of pain-avoidance in which we're led by circumstances rather than by Him. He says, *"Don't be like the horse and mule. They have no understanding. I want you to know that I will lead you. I will guide you with My eye. Just say 'yes' to Me."*

My wife, Cathy, raises horses. Her prize horse is a Tennessee Walker stallion named Black. When Black was in his prime, Cathy would just sit on his back and command, "Black, right," and the horse would turn right. When she said, "Black, walk," he would walk. And when she would say, "Black, stop," he would stop.

This well-trained horse would respond to Cathy's vocal commands with obedience. All he needed to hear was his master's voice speaking to him, and Black would respond by doing what Cathy expected him to do.

Learning to hear, to recognize the voice of our Lord Jesus, brings us into a life of joyful fulfillment as we make the daily decision to do what our Lord wants us to do.

The Holy Spirit broods over God's people, and He speaks a word to them. Jesus said, *"My sheep hear My voice, and I know them, and they follow Me"* (John 10:27).

This is what "the prayer God loves to answer" is all about.

## Methods of Prayer

To pray a good "yes" prayer, you need to be sure that you truly want God to intervene in your life and circumstances in order to bring about His dream for your life. You see, He loves a heart that believes in Him and believes Him. I can assure you beyond all shadow of doubt that God will always respond to your sincere "yes" prayer, because He knows it's spoken from your heart.

There are many rules and methods that have been put forth through the years about how to pray effectively. I have always had a hard time trying to master such formulas because they've seemed contrived and rote to me.

I've always wanted to know how to get God's attention and how to have the assurance that He likes my prayers and wants to answer them. After many years, it became clear to me that the most valid way to pray was to pray the prayer He wants me to pray.

Prayer is talking to God, nothing more. I can be happy when I talk to Him or I can be sad. I can be full of faith or full of garbage when I talk to Him. I can be in His will or in a pig pen when I talk to Him. The point is, no matter what is going on, I need to talk to Him.

The goal is to talk to God and pray the prayer He wants us to pray. He wants us to pray His "skeleton key prayer," in order to capture His dream for our lives.

## The Power of "Yes"

Saying "yes" to God releases His power from Heaven within us, around us, and on our behalf. It brings about His will in our lives and in the lives of those we pray for—and even extends to their loved ones. Our simple "yes" gives God an open door to work in our hearts and circumstances as well as in the hearts and circumstances of those around us.

The first time you agree with God during a challenging situation in your life, you may be praying in fear, desperation, anger, and even open sin, but the important thing is that you are saying "yes" to God, your heavenly Father. Your agreement with Him is a wonderful surrender to Him and is a very deep expression of worship to the One you trust more than you trust yourself.

When you do so, you will find that He will change you while He is changing the circumstances and situations you face. If repentance is needed, He will lead you to repentance. (See Romans 2:4.) As I said earlier, your agreement with Him releases the forces of Heaven to bring about the divine order that is needed in your life and circumstances.

## Ministering Angels

Angels are God's ministering spirits that He dispatches to help meet your needs. They are ministering to your needs even as you read this page. God's angels are there for you. He is not helping just a few special children of God. There are no favorites in God's family; He loves each of us equally, perfectly, and completely. He sends angels to you as well as to the pastor, the bishop, or the president of the United States. He loves us and cares for all equally.

The ministry of angels is for all. Your prayer of "yes" will release angels who will bring about miraculous occurrences in a marvelous display of other-dimensional power and resolve.

This spiritual power and resolve will calm the troubled seas of your life, heal the sick, raise the dead, give direction, and heal the hurting soul. This power regularly ignores the laws of physics, math, relativity, and all natural laws that are supposed to keep us earthbound but are unable to do so when God is at work. Angelic powers know your deepest needs and all your unspoken desires. They delight in making right all the wrongs and bringing a sense of real hope to even the most discouraged of God's people.

Praying the prayer that God loves to answer transfers the power of another, higher dimension to this earthly dimension in order to complete the dream God has dreamed for you. As our heavenly Father imposes His will over ours, hope is imparted to us, and we are reassured that there is One who is larger than us, One who knows better than we do.

When we walk with Him, we learn that He is not afraid to do what is best for us. He releases His angels to help us, and He works with us to build our individual lives as well as His kingdom on this planet.

God's dream for you is much grander than what you might expect. It is far greater than any office you may hold or any work or ministry you may do.

He won't stop coming after you until He hears you say "yes" to Him. He wants to see the dream He has dreamed for you—your divine destiny—come true. This means that you will have to hear Him with "new ears," the ears of your spirit, and see Him and His vision for you with "new eyes," the eyes of your spirit. It also requires a new heart—a heart that believes what your old heart could not believe, receives what your old heart could not receive, and dreams what your old heart could not dream.

As you sense His dream burning deeply within you, don't push it away. Don't be afraid of it. Simply agree with it and agree with Him. Your prayer should be, "Yes, Lord, I want to follow the dream You have for me."

## Catch God's Dream

The reason why many folks don't "catch" God's dream for them is because they are not certain they want to yield to His dream. God wants us to be willing workers with Him.

God loves you, forgives you, and has great dreams for you. Knowing this eradicates all fear from your heart.

Once, not long ago, while I was preaching in Albany, New York, I sensed that there was a dark cloud of guilt hovering over the congregation. This was not the brooding of the Holy Spirit; it was the condemnation of the enemy.

I felt led of God to begin my talk by raising some questions. I asked, "How many of you went through the five steps of the Plan of Salvation? How many of you prayed the Sinner's Prayer?" About 1,000 people were present, and almost 1,000 hands were in the air in response to my questions.

Next, I asked, "How many of you knew you were loved unconditionally and forgiven at that point when Jesus saved you?" Again, nearly every person's hand was raised.

I asked it a second time, and the hands went up again.

Realizing that many of these people were burdened with guilt, I changed my tactic and asked, "How many of you know, beyond all shadow of doubt, that you are loved unconditionally *now?*"

Amazingly, but not surprisingly, only about 150 hands went into the air! I knew then that I needed to show them from the Word that God loved them perfectly and unconditionally. It was my privilege to help them see that if God had truly forgiven them when they were His enemies, how much more would He forgive them now that they were His friends!

I told them about my own experience with guilt and condemnation and how I used to look down upon myself. They listened intently. I explained to them how the enemy had put them under condemnation because they had been "religionized" to such an extent that they could hardly cough without feeling guilty.

This is not God's dream for His children. Jesus died to set us free from all of that. My friends, John and Paula Sandford, have said that they feel a large part of their ministry is to evangelize "the unbelieving hearts of believers," and I understand where they're coming from with regard to that statement.

It seems as if the goal of many churches is to maintain the status quo, to preserve the system. In so doing, churches have replaced the Presence with the program and the Savior with the system. This always puts people under bondage and guilt, for the system is parasitical, drawing its very life from the people rather than the people finding life in God.

It is terrible to have God's people cower in fear at the sound of the voice of their loving heavenly Father. He loves, and He forgives. He knows that we are but grass. He knows our weaknesses because He made us. He forgives, He gathers, and He also dreams big dreams for the likes of you and me. And, I promise, He will never stop dreaming for you!

To catch God's dream we need to rise above the systems, the traditions, the doctrines, the dogmas, the programs, the denominations, and the buildings, and find the very Presence and life of God. Indeed, we need to rise into the heavenly places where we can see things, including ourselves and others, from God's point of view.

Let God dream His dream through you. Say "yes" to Him.

*"And all these blessings shall come upon you and overtake you, because you obey the voice of the Lord your God"* (Deuteronomy 28:2).

## SCRIPTURE REFERENCES FOR FURTHER STUDY

| | |
|---|---|
| Joshua 1:8 | Psalm 103:12 |
| Psalm 146:5 | 2 Corinthians 5:21 |
| 3 John 2 | John 8:32 |
| Matthew 5:6 | Psalm 3:3 |
| Philippians 4:19 | Psalm 119:105 |
| John 14:21 | Philippians 4:13 |
| Isaiah 26:3 | Ephesians 6:10 |

Paul wrote, *"For all the promises of God in Him are Yes, and in Him Amen, to the glory of God through us"* (2 Corinthians 1:20).

CHAPTER FOUR

*Entering the "Yes" of God*

In the preceding chapters we have seen that *agreeing with God* brings more than answered prayer; it brings God's direct involvement into our lives. His intervention in our lives leads us to experience one success after another and one good thing after another, simply because we are agreeing with Him and asking Him to take control of our lives.

Our saying "yes" to the Lord invites Him to come into our lives in all His fullness. When we do so we are asking Him to accomplish many things in our lives: to work in our circumstances, our hearts, and our minds and to arrange (or rearrange) things in our lives so His purposes can be fulfilled.

In Chapter 3 we learned about the dream God has dreamed for us. The prophet Jeremiah gives us some insight into that wonderful dream: *"For I know the thoughts that I think toward you, says the Lord, thoughts of peace and not of evil, to give you a future and a hope. Then you will call upon Me and go and pray to Me, and I will listen to you. And you will seek Me and find Me, when you search for Me with all your heart"* (Jer. 29:11-13).

God has wonderful things in store for you, and, as you learn to pray the prayer He loves to answer (with blind faith in His goodness, if necessary), you will soon discover that He listens to you when you pray, and you will come to realize the future and the hope that He has set in place for you.

You will discover that it is no longer necessary to complain to Him about your circumstances or to beg Him for what you want. Instead, you will say "yes" to Him, fully realizing that He is always there, and He will work things out in the best possible way, both because He loves you and because He wants, probably more than we do, for His dream to come to pass.

Though His ways and thoughts are higher than yours, your agreement with Him will help "bridge the gap" between your ways and His ways, your thoughts and His thoughts, and probably, most importantly, your will and His will. Even though you don't understand all God's ways and plans, you can still say "yes" to Him by faith.

God says that as you do so, *"I will be found by you...and I will bring you back from your captivity"* (Jer. 29:14).

This, in large measure, is what I mean by "entering the 'yes' of God."

## *"How Long Will God Dream a Dream for You?"*

I was speaking on "Entering the 'Yes' of God" when I was ministering in Pescara, Italy, in 2004. An elderly Pentecostal pastor was sitting in the front row. I had met him before the meeting, and he had proudly announced to me, "I am ninety-three years old!"

As I spoke that evening, I watched him and noticed how this faithful servant of the Cross was listening so intently to my words. I was talking about the dream God has dreamed for us and how we can release this dream by simply saying "yes" to the Lord.

I explained, "Even when we do not know what God's dream for us is, our praying 'yes' releases the activity of Heaven that brings His dream to pass. Angels are sent on assignment to prepare circumstances and hearts so that every door that needs to open will open indeed."

I glanced down at the old pastor as I spoke and noticed that his eyes were filled with tears. My heart overflowed with compassion for him, and I felt certain that he would have a question for me at the end of the service.

In fact, I grew a bit preoccupied in anticipation of his question, and so I asked God for wisdom to enable me to answer him in the most correct and encouraging way possible. After the meeting, as I had thought he would, the white-haired gentleman took hold of the interpreter's arm and approached me.

His question was one I had not anticipated, however. With quivering lips, he asked, "Pastor Don, how long will God dream a dream for you?"

The moment he asked this, my spirit filled with thoughts of all his years of faithful ministry to the Body of Christ. I knew he had played a vital part in what God wanted to do and was doing in the nation of Italy.

I could sense that now his heart was struggling with feelings of uselessness. I could see deep into his heart where he was wondering if he could be of any further use to the cause of God's kingdom in these, the final days of his life.

God, in His great faithfulness, had let me see into this dear man's heart, and my own heart filled with love and compassion for him, as these words flowed from my mouth, "As long as you breathe, God dreams His dreams for you, and He will take you from one adventure to the next. He is never finished with you, for even after you have breathed your last breath on this earth, you will praise Him for all eternity before His throne in Heaven!"

He reached out and embraced me, holding me tightly for several minutes as if he was laying his heart on my heart. He wept for a long time, and so did I. No more praying was necessary, and no further prophetic word was needed, for the Lord

Himself was comforting, encouraging, and empowering this man of God, so that he would respond afresh to the One he had so deeply loved and faithfully served for so many years!

He was reentering the "yes" of God.

God is looking for a people who will respond to the sound of His voice as this man did. It is the most exciting experience any human being can ever have.

## What Is God Saying to You?

God is speaking to you.

God knows your name.

God knows the plans He has for you.

He's the One who made you.

He's the One who called you. He wants to lead you by the sound of His voice, so you can do what He has called you to do.

It doesn't matter how old you are or how young you are. Things like age, appearance, background, education, religious training, and economic status are not the issue. Those things matter little in the Kingdom of God. What really matters is your willingness to agree with His dream for you. He wants your prayer to be simply, "Yes, Lord!"

God is actually waiting for people who will agree with Him. Do you hear His voice? Are you responding to His voice?

Again, regardless of your age, your finances, or even your heartache, God still holds His dream for you in His outstretched hands, and He is anticipating the moment when you will turn to Him and say, "Yes."

## *Entering the Most Holy Place Is Entering the "Yes" of God*

A tabernacle is a place where man meets with God. In the Old Testament Tabernacle (the Tabernacle of Moses), God revealed Himself to His people.

The Tabernacle of Moses consisted of three main divisions: the outer court, the inner court (the Holy Place), and the Holy of Holies (the Most Holy Place). These three sections each had unique characteristics and purposes in ancient times; and even today they have significance and relevance as they depict different levels and aspects of our relationship with God.

The outer court of the Tabernacle was the place where sacrifices were made in an effort to find God's forgiveness and cleansing. Today, people who are in the outer court (figuratively speaking) live lives that are totally self-centered. While there, these people are still focused on doing things for their own benefit, and they have no concept that anything is from God.

Their kingdom is the "kingdom of self," not the Kingdom of God, and all their desires are self-centered and focused on the fulfillment of their selfish desires.

It is a fleshy realm, a place where man strives to be in charge of his own life. Instead of enjoying the benefits of the Kingdom of God, the person in the outer court is focused on the struggles and conflicts that are part and parcel of the self-life.

The next division of the Tabernacle is the inner court, or the Holy Place. In this division of the Tabernacle, man is not really sure who he is or what he wants to be. Somehow, he knows he is supposed to be involved with the building of God's Kingdom, but he wants to build his own kingdom at the same time.

The man in the Holy Place hears God telling him to do things, but he still wants to do things for himself. Therefore, it is a place of conflict, struggle, and mixture for him even though he sees items of gold representing the gifts and qualities of God all around him.

The Most Holy Place (the Holy of Holies) was where God manifested His Presence to the High Priest. It was a wonderful place of mercy, grace, blessing, and love.

The power of the Most Holy Place (the Presence of God) is love, for God is love (see 1 John 4:8), and if you are in His Presence, you are enveloped by His love, and your heart responds to His love with love. It is there that you know that the most excellent way of all (see 1 Cor. 12:31) is to love God with all your heart, soul, mind, and strength and to love your neighbor as yourself (see Matt. 22:37-39).

Love, in the Most Holy Place, is the atmosphere in which you live and move and have your being. (See Acts 17:28.)

The Most Holy Place is a place of relationship where the believer draws close to God and God draws close to the believer. Oswald Chambers, in *My Utmost for His Highest*, writes:

> We do not know what God's compelling purpose is, but whatever happens, we must maintain our relationship with Him. We must never allow anything to damage our relationship with God, but if something does damage it, we must take the time to make it right again.
>
> The most important aspect of Christianity is not the work we do, but the relationship we maintain and the surrounding influence and qualities produced by that relationship. That is all God asks us to give our attention to, and it is the one thing that is continually under attack.

Maintaining our vital relationship with God involves entering His presence and staying there. This is the wonderful benefit of being in the "yes" of God.

Many Christians talk about the power to heal, to cast out devils, and to raise the dead, but not as many talk about the power of love. If you pray for somebody in an effort to demonstrate the power to heal, you will miss the point. It is God's great love for the person that compels Him to move through you to bring healing to another. Jesus was moved with compassion. It was always out of His loving compassion that He ministered love, healing, and hope to the people.

You can search for the gift of God and the gifts of the Holy Spirit and still fall short of His glory. The issue in God's heart is not how well you can impart His gifts, but how completely you let Him love the world through you.

When we let God love the world through us many amazing things take place. As co-laborers with Him, we learn that He heals because He loves and He blesses because He loves. When we allow Him to move through us, we will love the world as He does, and we will scatter the seed of the Gospel freely everywhere.

In the Most Holy Place, we trust the Lord to take the seed wherever He wants it to go, and we understand that the more seed we scatter, the more seed we will have. This is a law of the Kingdom of God. In fact, you learn there that you will never run out of seed.

The compassionate love of God drives us to reckless abandonment in our pursuit of Him as we carry the seed of His love to the four corners of the world.

There is a penetration of the Spirit of God that needs to occur within us, for this is what leads us to agree with God. The walls of resistance that we have built around our lives through the years need to come down. That will happen only in the Most Holy Place—in the Manifest Presence of God. Here, we are humbled. Here, we relinquish our struggle to Him who alone has the power and compassion to bring us into our destiny.

The Lord is the only one who has the power to change our thoughts, our mind, and our desires. We cannot make these changes on our own. He puts His truth against our lies, His life against our religious resistance, and His compassion against our flapping tongues.

Our tongues often become unruly, as the Book of James points out. Through slander, lies, gossip, accusations, and back-biting, relationships and people are destroyed. Only the Manifest Presence of God can tame and control the human tongue.

Likewise, the Manifest Presence of God can turn our faithlessness into faithfulness.

God's plan and desire for you is to get you to the place where you will say an unqualified "yes" to Him, no matter what. He wants to hear you say, "Lord, You can have me, change me, and do with me whatever You want to do."

From then on you will know and experience the joy of the Lord, which is your strength. (See Nehemiah 8:10.) The joy of the Lord is found within the Manifest Presence of God. The joy of the Lord is in the "yes" of God.

## Building the Kingdom

Whose kingdom are you building? Are you building God's Kingdom or your own?

In the Presence of God (the Most Holy Place) we learn that the Lord is not restricted by how someone looks or how much money a person can put in the offering plate. There we discover that God is not concerned about the kind of clothing people wear. He never discriminates according to any earthly traits.

Instead, our God is concerned with the human heart. He does not look upon exterior things, but on the things of the spirit. (See First Samuel 16:7.) He never shows any partiality whatsoever.

God wants to pour His love through us, so that His Kingdom can be built through us, on earth. This is the kind of God we serve—a God of love, compassion, mercy, and grace. This is the One we meet and get to know in the Most Holy Place. When our gifts and anointing are used to build our own kingdom, we thwart His work in us and in the earth.

He is a gathering God, One who always gathers and never scatters. He calls us to Himself, and He does not send us away.

God is building His own Kingdom. Unlike the kingdoms of man, His Kingdom has no walls or fences. When you are building God's Kingdom, you are sowing the seeds of His love freely wherever you go, and your goal is to reach as many people as possible, knowing that the harvest will be reaped at just the right time, His time.

If a field is not seeded, there will be no harvest. Our job is to seed the field. In the outer court, people *eat* the seed. In the holy place, people *plant* seeds very carefully, close to them, one at a time, because they are still focused on building their own kingdom. They still want to maintain control.

In the Most Holy Place, however, we do not eat the seed, nor do we plant the seed close to us. Rather, we *sow* the seed, broadcasting it and trusting in the Lord to take it wherever He wants it to go. Then the wind of the Holy Spirit can and will blow the seed to the four corners of the earth.

In the Most Holy Place, you understand that the more seed you sow, the more seed you will have. In fact, when you're seeding the nations, you will never run out of seed!

There's no need to keep a record there of how many people you've led to the Lord, because you are building God's Kingdom, not your own. Your job is just to sow the seed, realizing that it will take root and grow, and the Lord will reap the harvest. Perhaps you will get involved in the reaping of the harvest as well, but you're comfortable in knowing that this is entirely up to the Lord.

When the harvest is ready, you may find yourself in a different field than the one you planted, a field where someone else planted the seed, and you will be called to help in the harvest of that field. As you learn to dwell in God's Presence, you realize that these things don't matter anymore. All that matters is that His Kingdom, never man's, never yours, is built. Determining to live in the "yes" of God transfers your desire to His plan, His dream, and His desire for you and for those whose lives you touch each day.

## The "Yes" of God

As we've pointed out, the outer court is the place of "all man"—self-centeredness—and the Holy Place is the place of mixture. The Most Holy Place, however, is the place of "all God." It is a place of separation unto the Lord and purity. This is the realm of the "yes" of God, where God's will is done and God's Kingdom is built.

In the Most Holy Place, we abandon ourselves to Him, so that He can build His kingdom in us and through us. This is the place of total surrender, the holy realm of agreement—the place where we enjoy His Presence and His purposes. In His Presence we find fullness of joy and pleasures forevermore. (See Psalm 16:11.)

In the Holy Place, the place of mixture, we see the golden candlesticks, the golden altar of incense, and the bread of God's Presence. Through these symbols, God is showing us many things about Himself; we learn, for example, that Jesus is the Light of the World, the Bread of Life, and we discover that His prayers, like incense, rise to God as intercessions in our behalf.

In effect, the furniture of the Holy Place helps us see who Jesus is, but we see only in part, the various parts and pieces that are represented by the items we find there. We learn about the gifts of the Holy Spirit there, as well, but still we don't have the total picture.

In the Most Holy Place, the realm of "all God," the pieces of the puzzle are put together for us, and we begin the journey of fully understanding who God is. It is there that we are broken into "pieces," and in our brokenness before Him, all we can do is cry, "Yes, Father."

Stated another way, in the Holy Place, Jesus is broken down into pieces we can understand. But in the Most Holy Place, God breaks us down into pieces He can use.

Really, the Christian life is not all that complicated, but we try to make it so. We turn it into a seemingly endless list of rules and regulations involving how we dress, how many times we should attend services, what we should eat and drink, and so forth. We judge others according to those rules, and we thereby greatly complicate our lives and, in the process, theirs as well.

God simply wants to break us so that all that remains in us is the humble cry of "yes." When we pray the prayer He loves to answer, He takes control of our lives, and His will begins to be accomplished in us and through us. It is then that we begin to hear Him speaking directly to us.

He's bringing us to Himself, so He can live His life through us. He just wants us to respond to Him. This is truly entering the "yes" of God.

## On Earth as It Is in Heaven

God wants His will to be done on earth as it is in Heaven. This is clear by the way He taught us to pray. But this can only be accomplished through His people. Remember, His will is already being done in Heaven. If His will is to be done on earth and if His dream for humanity is to come to pass, there must be people all over the world who will let Him live His life through them. There must be those who will yield totally to Him. There must be those who simply and quietly agree with their heavenly Father, no matter what the human cost.

But even this conversation is from a human perspective. Many times we talk as though God always gives us things to do that will be very painful and dreadful. We act as though God tells us to do things without regard to what is best for us over the long term. We seem to yield to His plan as a last resort, after trying every other earthly means to do what we want to do. We often act as though He does not have our best interest at heart. But nothing could be further from the truth. God's dream for us will bring the greatest satisfaction imaginable. It will be fulfilling and complete. His dream will cause us to leap from bed each morning with the exciting expectation of what is in store for us as we live day by day, moment by moment, for Him.

God is so big, and yet He loves us so much that He wants us to know His will and also to do His will. He really does want to reveal His will to us; it does not have to be a mystery to us any longer.

However, He has given His people a free will of their own. He will never force or impose His will upon us. He wants us, of our own free will, to respond to Him, so we will be able to have fellowship with Him, serve Him, and honor Him.

The rule and reign of God that exists in Heaven will become manifest on earth through the lives of people who willingly pray "yes" to Him.

## *"Get to Europe Immediately"*

A few years ago, at a prayer meeting in our Destiny Image facility in Shippensburg, Pennsylvania, the Holy Spirit spoke to my heart. He said, *"You need to get to Europe immediately."*

Then He told me what I would be preaching when I got to Italy. He wanted me to share the insights He had given to me about surrendering our wills to His.

I spoke this to the group who had gathered with us as soon as we were done praying. My wife, Cathy, had heard the same thing. Dan Cutrona, who often traveled with me and ministered with me, also had heard the same thing!

When our hearts are turned to Him so fully that "yes" is always on our lips, amazing things always happen. When He wants us to do something, we must begin to respond with heart-felt submission to His will, no matter what other things we might have planned to do.

God was calling us, and we knew we had to say "yes" to Him, so we entered the "yes" of God, and the results were truly glorious. We went to Italy and had phenomenal meetings with God's people there.

So, by this time, I am sure you are hearing God's voice. Do not hesitate to enter the "yes" of God and experience the most exciting adventure of your life! Live in His Presence and let Him love you and love the world through you. You will be letting Him build His kingdom right here on earth.

*Jesus said, "But seek first the kingdom of God and His righteousness, and all these things shall be added to you"* **(Matthew 6:33).**

Yes, and Amen!

## SCRIPTURE REFERENCES FOR FURTHER STUDY

| | |
|---|---|
| Jeremiah 33:3 | John 16:13 |
| Isaiah 43:21 | Romans 4:20-21 |
| Colossians 1:10 | 1 Thessalonians 5:24 |
| Psalm 111:10 | John 7:17 |
| James 1:5 | John 9:31 |
| Psalm 32:8 | Philippians 2:13 |
| Proverbs 16:3 | |

Jesus said, *"But let your 'Yes' be 'Yes,' and your 'No,' 'No.' For whatever is more than these is from the evil one"* (Matthew 5:37).

# CHAPTER FIVE

# Let Your "Yes" Be "Yes"

In *How to Obtain Fullness of Power*, E.M. Bounds writes, "There are many people greatly puzzled because their prayers never seem to reach the ear of God, but fall back, unanswered, to the earth. There is no mystery about it. It is because they have not met the one great, fundamental condition of prevailing prayer—a surrendered will and a surrendered life. It is when we make God's will ours, that He makes our will His."

This what Jesus means when He tells us to let our "yes" be "yes." This is vitally important teaching from the heart of our Master. It is clear that He wants us to say "yes" to Him, but our "yes" needs to be far more than just lip service; it must be the central focus of our lives. For our "yes" to be "yes," it must be lived and believed, not just spoken, and our lives and wills must be surrendered fully to Him.

So, "yes" is far more than just a word. Indeed, it is more than just a prayer. It is a lifestyle commitment and an attitude of heart that perseveres in agreement with God and His dream for you, no matter what the negative people and negative circumstances around you might declare.

To let your "yes" be "yes," you must be strong in believing that God will always do what's best for you. As a "yes" believer, you will walk by faith, not by sight, always trusting in the Lord, seeking to abide in His presence, and endeavoring to follow the dream He has for you.

There are really only two responses to God and His will; they are either "yes" or "no." There is no middle ground, no gray area. You either affirm the will of God in your life, or you deny Him and His will. Even when you do not understand what the will of God is, your willingness to agree with His will opens the doors of opportunity and possibility that can come in no other way.

I know that there are some who insist that you must know the will of God before you can trust Him for it. But that is only true when you do not believe God has only His best ready for you.

When you begin to understand that God's dream is the happiest, the most fulfilled, and the most effective life you can live, it will become easier to rest in Him, especially when you don't have a real clue about His plans for you.

## We Are "Under Construction"

When you say "yes" to the Lord, your life becomes a cleared building site—His property, if you will. In other words, you are under construction. He has purchased you so that He might be able to live within you and build His Kingdom in you and through you. To Him, therefore, you are valuable "real estate."

When you allow yourself to be His building site, you will then be willing for Him to clear your heart, gently and lovingly removing all those things that are no longer important to you or Him. He is preparing a habitation for Himself within you.

Paul writes, *"Or do you not know that your body is the temple of the Holy Spirit who is in you, whom you have from God, and you are not your own? For you were bought at a price; therefore glorify God in your body and in your spirit, which are God's"* (1 Cor. 6:19-20).

When you say "yes" to God, you do not belong to yourself any longer. You are purposefully laying aside your will, believing that His will is far better than yours. You are embracing His dream for you. You are His, and, as His possession, He can now begin the most exciting time of your life. He is now beginning to build you and to lead you into your destiny.

For Him to build His Kingdom within you, God understandably removes all existing structures that you had built while you were constructing your own personal kingdom. He will clear the landscape of your heart, leaving it completely bare, ready to have His foundation and building put on your site. He will mercifully go deep into your life so as to remove everything that's old, decaying, and useless. Even the old foundation upon which your life was built may need to be adjusted or even removed so it can be rebuilt in His way and according to His dream for you.

He wants to build a house of His own choosing, a building not made with human hands, but one in which He will live and give you true fulfillment every day of your life. His work is always powerful and unique. In a very real sense, we are still being fearfully and wonderfully made!

## God-Possessed

The Holy Spirit lives within you. This means that you are a God-possessed person.

As such, God is calling you to a higher place in the Spirit, a place where you can hear His voice, experience an ever-deepening faith, and enjoy His providence, favor, and provision wherever you are.

This is the Most Holy Place that I referred to earlier—the place where you will have fellowship with the Father and hear Him speaking to you, waiting for you to respond in full surrender with His will.

I remember a time when Jonathan and Donald, my two oldest sons, were seven and five years old, and their mother was in the kitchen baking chocolate chip cookies. The boys were watching her, as she pulled the freshly baked treats out of the oven.

I'm sure the boys were enjoying the sight and smell of the cookies, and they were surely anticipating their taste. Cathy put the baking tray on the counter and said, "Don't touch the cookies, Boys. They are too hot!"

"Okay, Mommy!" they said.

She stepped out of the kitchen for a moment, and the boys headed right to the cookies! Needless to say, they burnt their fingertips and began to cry. It was a lesson they needed to learn only once, for the next time Cathy made cookies, she pulled the tray out of the oven, and Jonathan asked, "Are the trays hot?"

"Yes, very hot," she replied.

"Will you tell me when they're cool enough?" was his next question.

Jonathan and Donald had learned their lesson, but it was a hard, pain-filled lesson that would not have been necessary had they simply listened to their mother's voice and responded with a true "yes" from their hearts. They had said "yes," but they did not truly mean it. In actuality, their "yes" had been a "no."

When we say "yes" to the Father, we must do so with a willing heart, one that wants to do what He tells us to do.

Paul writes, *"I beseech you therefore, brethren, by the mercies of God, that you present your bodies a living sacrifice, holy, acceptable to God, which is your reasonable service. And do not be conformed to this world, but be transformed by the renewing of your mind, that you may prove what is that good and acceptable and perfect will of God"* (Rom. 12:1-2).

Presenting your whole life to God as a living sacrifice is truly a reasonable service to Him in light of all His mercies to you. Offering yourself to Him completely is a resounding "yes" to Him that is heard throughout Heaven. It reaches His heart with the sweetness of honey and the innocence of a newborn child. It is then that you will discover and begin to live His perfectly wonderful dream for your life.

## Weakness Does Not Disqualify

You must never allow your human weakness to disqualify you for what God has planned for you. Your failures do not prove that you are wicked; they simply prove that you are human. Though you are filled with God, it's important to remember that you are a human being who is filled with God.

That's why you need to enter and stay in the "yes" of God, for there you will be refined, strengthened, healed, taught, and made whole in every way.

Run *to* God, not *away* from Him, when you fail. Paul said, *"And He said to me, 'My grace is sufficient for you, for My strength is made perfect in weakness.' Therefore most gladly I will rather boast in my infirmities, that the power of Christ may rest upon me. Therefore I take pleasure in infirmities, in reproaches, in needs, in persecutions, in distresses, for Christ's sake. For when I am weak, then I am strong"* (2 Cor. 12:9-10).

Paul was a man who knew he had weaknesses, but he used his weaknesses as a sign that he had to run to the Lord for strength. Religion, on the other hand, causes people to run away from God when they fail, due to guilt and shame. God, however, wants us to run to Him, so He can continue His work in our lives.

## Weakness or Strength?

How could Paul make such a statement as this: "When I am weak, then I am strong"? It doesn't seem to make much sense, does it? But the answer is simple. The weakest part of Paul became the strongest part of him because he confessed his weakness and asked the Lord to make it strong. Over time, therefore, his weak points became his strong points.

Weakness and failure never stopped Paul. What they did was teach him to pray. He did not allow weakness to disqualify him for what God had in store for him. He chose not to live in guilt. He found forgiveness through simple repentance and then he kept on moving forward.

He proclaimed, *"There is therefore now no condemnation to those who are in Christ Jesus, who do not walk according to the flesh, but according to the Spirit"* (Rom. 8:1).

We need to say the same thing to ourselves whenever we struggle with weakness and failure. It is critical that we understand this. The enemy accuses us and causes us to look at the part of us that still needs to be healed. The Holy Spirit, on the other hand, causes us to look at the parts of us that do function properly and that are doing exactly what God wants them to do.

When we see our weakness, it should remind us to pray the "skeleton key prayer" to the Father, to repent of our sins, and to surrender our lives to Him afresh. Wholeness comes as we learn to respond to Him in these ways. Healing comes as we surrender our wills to His.

God is actively involved in your life in so many different ways. There is nothing about you that He does not already know. He is not surprised by your failures. He knows your weaknesses, but He still loves you and wants you to get back "on track" again and follow Him.

## Yes, Yes, Yes!

As the daily pressures of life press in upon us, it is often difficult to remember that the Lord is a living Being inside of us. We tend to forget too easily that He has a mind of His own, a will of His own, and desires of His own.

He wants so much for us to yield ourselves to Him so He can live His life through us. He is not interested in our "looking spiritual," whatever that means. Nor is He interested in having us act spiritual.

Our God wants our "yes" to be "yes." He doesn't want us to pretend that He is inside of us. He doesn't want us to be religious either. He wants us to give up all that fleshy stuff and give our lives to Him in complete submission to His Lordship.

God wants us to stop *trying* to be Christians. Instead, He wants us to give ourselves to Him, so He can do in us whatever He wants to do. The problem in all this, however, is that we're used to doing things in certain ways that need changing. We often have habits of thought, religion, practice, and feeling that are opposed to God and His ways.

He wants you to be willing to change. As you learn to look at Him as He truly is, everything will begin to change. Of course, I am assuming that you are willing to allow Him to change you! My guess is that since you have come this far in this book, your heart is open and soft to Him, and your greatest desire is to simply relax and let Him do His work in you and through you.

God is immeasurably great. The Psalmist said, *"Great is the Lord, and greatly to be praised"* (Ps. 48:1).

He is greater than our habit patterns, greater than our denominations, greater than our philosophies, greater than our education, and greater than our experience. He is greater than our lifestyle as well. If we allow Him to do so, He will show us how great He is, and He will give us opportunities that we cannot possibly imagine.

So, ask God to give you the courage to say "no" to your own ways, doctrines, limitations, and fears. He will help you say "no" to the ways of this world and the things of the past, and He will make all things new in your life.

To let your "yes" be "yes," then, is to let your life be conformed to His will. This is what Paul is saying in his letter to the Romans: *"And do not be conformed to this world, but be transformed by the renewing of your mind, that you may prove what is that good and acceptable and perfect will of God"* (Romans 12:2).

## *The Written Word or the Living Word?*

There is a big difference between the written Word and the living Word. We can manipulate the written Word to fit into our own plans and desires. Likewise, we can interpret the written Word in a variety of ways.

Some people, for example, interpret some verses from the Bible as meaning that women should never talk in church, wear makeup or jewelry, or ever wear slacks. Other people interpret other verses as meaning that one should not go to a movie, dance, watch television, or have instrumental music in services.

I think you get the idea. We need the living Word of God—the Lord Jesus Christ—to guide us in understanding His written Word. We need to hear Him speak to our hearts. We need to dwell in His Manifest Presence. The living Word cannot be manipulated. For the Lord Himself acts according to the counsel of His own will, which the written Word reflects. When the living Word acts in a way that is contrary to what we believe the written Word says, we must understand that the living Word is not beholding to our doctrines, He is only beholding to Himself. In the Most Holy Place, His Manifest Presence, He cannot be manipulated, for this is the realm of "all God." Here, we see Him as He is and we are instructed in the ways of the living Word Himself.

Jesus said, *"But the Helper, the Holy Spirit, whom the Father will send in My name, He will teach you all things, and bring to your remembrance all things that I said to you"* (John 14:26). Let the Holy Spirit teach you and guide you into all truth.

One time not long ago I was scheduled to go to London. It was during a period of great personal turmoil, so I ended up not being able to go. However, I sent a friend in my place who also happened to be named Don. Since all this came about at the last minute, communication between my office and London broke down.

My secretary had given my description to the person who was going to meet me at the Heathrow airport. She told him that I was a big guy with a beard and a ponytail and that I wore glasses. Perhaps she also said I looked a little weird!

Certainly, with that description in his mind, I should have been easy to spot. However, the person who went to London was another Don, but he was quite the opposite of me! He was a thin man with short hair, no beard, no ponytail, and no glasses. The one and only obvious similarity between us was our name!

He got off the plane, recovered his luggage, and began looking for the one who was supposed to take him to the hotel. Almost everyone else had gone before he noticed a man who appeared to be waiting for someone. Don took note of the man's puzzled facial expression and how he scratched his head as he was reading the scrap of paper he clutched tightly in his hand.

My friend walked up to the Englishman and said, "Excuse me, are you waiting for somebody from Destiny Image by any chance?"

"Yes, I am."

"Well, I'm the one you're waiting for."

"What? It can't be true. This note says you're a big man with a ponytail and a beard and glasses! You cannot possibly be the one I am looking for!"

Eventually they reached an understanding and Don was able to go with him, but the interesting thing is that the Englishman was bound to the written word instead of believing what his eyes were showing him and his ears were telling him. He initially chose to say "yes" to the written word and "no" to the living word. Only after much conversation was he able to believe the living reality rather than what was written on the paper.

Many Christians are the same way. Even if living proof seemingly contradicts the written Word (or their interpretation of that Word), they become resistant. Many times they will even grow adamant, refusing to change.

Please don't get me wrong. I believe in the Bible. In fact, I love the written Word of God. I have eight different versions of the Scriptures, and I read and study them daily. I believe the Word of God, and I believe that God has never violated His Word.

He is always true to His Word, and He cannot lie. He never goes against His Word. However, every day He will violate what *my* personal interpretation is when it does not accurately represent the reality of the living Word! God is not bound to act according to what I believe about Him. Rather, we are bound to believe Him as He demonstrates Himself to us.

I want to experience the living Word. My fellowship is never with the letter of the Word, because I know that the letter kills. This is not heresy. My relationship is not with a book; it is with Jesus Christ, who is revealed in the Book. The living Spirit of the Word imparts life to me. (See Second Corinthians 3:6.)

## *Eyes Have Not Seen*

The apostle Paul quoted the prophet Isaiah, who wrote, *"Eye has not seen, nor ear heard, nor have entered into the heart of man the things which God has prepared for those who love Him"* (1 Cor. 2:9).

He then went on to explain, *"But God has revealed them to us through His Spirit. For the Spirit searches all things, yes, the deep things of God"* (1 Cor. 2:10).

This is a beautiful description of the difference between adhering to the written Word and responding to the living Word. Believing that God has prepared each for me makes me wake up every day with a renewed sense of wonder and anticipation—because I realize that each new day is an opportunity to experience the living Presence of Jesus, as He leads me step by step and reveals Himself and His ways to me.

The Holy Spirit reveals the deep things of God to us, and I want to hear His voice speaking to me and showing me those wonderful, deep things. I am not happy with anything less than the Manifest Presence of God.

When I stand behind a pulpit, I cannot just preach a sermon—a written, well-polished treatise that I've prepared for the people. I just can't do it that way anymore. If I don't know that the living Presence of Almighty God is speaking through me, I don't have anything to say to the people. To speak to folks without the knowledge that God has something to say to them through me, at that moment, is grossly unfair to the people and leaves them and me unfulfilled, not to mention all the wasted time involved!

Our Lord has a lot to say to us. But He will mostly speak to us Spirit to spirit. He will give us ample opportunity to agree with Him and His plan, if we will get out of the way. This is how we can hear His voice.

He has more for us than we can possibly imagine, so when He speaks, it will most often be outside of our comfort zone as well as beyond what our religious instruction permits. We need to quiet our hearts and listen to Him, the One who is waiting to lead us into the most wondrous adventures of our lives.

When you hear Him, your response should naturally be, "Yes, Lord!" This allows Heaven to open its doors and manipulate circumstances so as to do what He is showing you to do. If He can part the Red Sea, He can make His own way through the systems and struggles of the world in order to accomplish the dream He has most certainly dreamed for you!

*"He who calls you is faithful, who also will do it"* **(1 Thessalonians 5:24).**

## SCRIPTURE REFERENCES FOR FURTHER STUDY

Galatians 2:20  
Isaiah 55:11  
1 Corinthians 2:9-10  
2 Corinthians 3:6  

Psalm 48:1-2  
Romans 12:1-2  
Matthew 5:37

John writes, *"And the Word became flesh and dwelt among us, and we beheld His glory, the glory as of the only begotten of the Father, full of grace and truth"* (John 1:14).

# CHAPTER SIX

# Possessed by Jesus

The Word of God became flesh and lived among us. His name is Jesus, He lives within us, and we are possessed by Him. Yes, I said *possessed*. We are filled, consumed, saturated, drenched, "Spirit-logged," and possessed by Him. He is full of grace and truth, therefore, so are we.

We were bought and paid for by His blood. Now we are His personal love, His consuming desire, His forever bride. We need only to respond to this awesome relationship to see the wondrous possibilities inherent in such a union.

For this to unfold in our lives, the Word needs to become flesh—the living Word to us—not just letters arranged into words, words arranged into sentences, but the living Word, the Lord Jesus Himself, must become flesh. It is better to have one verse of the Bible become flesh (a living Word) to us than to memorize 100 verses without any of them being truly alive for us.

The living Word, the Lord Jesus Christ, wants to become flesh in us, and He wants us to give ourselves to Him so that He can live His life through us. Indeed, He is looking for people who will let Him change the world through them.

He is looking for those who will take Him to the four corners of the earth through them. He is looking for someone to take Him into the classrooms and someone else to take Him into the halls of government.

He wants folks like you and me to take Him into the factory and the grocery store. He is needed in the television newsroom and in the offices of businesses, large and small. He is waiting for someone to take Him wherever there is a human being who is looking for something more than what he or she has experienced before. He does not require us to preach or to pass out Gospel tracts, He simply waits for us to yield to Him so that He—Jesus Himself—can love the world through us.

Remember, you are possessed. You are His property.

Jesus came into my life with His own mind, desires, goals, power, and ability. Therefore, it is accurate to say that I am truly possessed by a "foreign entity," a life form that is not from our dimension or universe. He is not of this earth, but I can certainly feel Him inside of me. His attributes reside within me, therefore, as well. Jesus said, *"All authority has been given to Me in heaven and on earth"* (Matt. 28:18).

That supernatural authority is within Him, and He lives within us! This means that all authority in Heaven and on earth dwells within us! Full spiritual authority and power are available to all who will pray "yes" to God, truly submitting their wills to God's will.

This kind of prayer will not work as a means of getting what we want, however. It is not a bargaining tool. Our sincere prayer to the Lord, yielding our hearts and lives to Him, releases His plan and His dream for our lives. We are the ones who must trust Him, that His desires for us will be personally fulfilling and satisfying.

Praying the prayer God loves to answer truly releases all the power of Heaven to arrange and rearrange the circumstances of our lives according to God's plan for us. Resisting this process is counter-productive. How can we resist what we have agreed to? How can we say "no" to the path He puts us on after we have said "yes" to the destination?

In *God's Will: Our Dwelling Place,* Andrew Murray writes, "When the Christian learns to see God's will in everything that happens to him—grievous or pleasing, great or small—the prayer, *Thy will be done,* will become the unceasing expression of adoring submission and praise....The soul will taste the rest and the bliss of knowing that it is always encircled and watched over by God's will."

## The Power Within Must Come Out

Jesus is able to do things that I can't even imagine. As I pray to Him with a heart that is filled with adoration and agreement, I realize more fully than ever that He is *"...able to do exceedingly abundantly above all that we ask or think, according to the power that works in us"* (Eph. 3:20).

His power—a power and ability that are not from our limited, earthly dimension—is at work within you. Jesus wants His power to find an outlet through you so that He can reach others through you.

As you let Him possess your life in the fullest possible way, His power and ability will become a river of life flowing out of you to all those you come in contact with every day. You do not have to try to make this happen any more than you have to try to remember to breathe, for it becomes the automatic response of your spirit to God.

Breathing is a natural function of our bodies, unless there is something that interrupts the natural process. The love and power of God also flow from us both supernaturally and naturally. It happens without us thinking about it, as almost an involuntary response.

Your mere presence should change the atmosphere of the room you are in without a word, a song, or a prayer. Your smile, your touch, your compassion, and your joy are the conduits through which the Presence and power of God flow, even when you are not aware of it. This is why giving ourselves afresh to Him every day is the most powerful "habit" we can ever develop.

Our Lord is waiting to display His wonders from a higher dimension through you, into your family, neighborhood, place of employment, community, church, surrounding areas, and even the world.

I often hear Him speaking to me. He says, *"Give yourself to Me. Let Me work through you. Let Me change the world through you."*

In response, I cry, "Yes, Lord."

He continues by telling me to set His people free, to bless, to give someone a hug. I do not have to think about doing these things; as His life flows through me, those around me are touched, encouraged, even changed.

God is actually looking for people who will carry His Presence to others. Your simple touch carries the substance of Spirit that heals the sick and strengthens the weary. Your touch can be the way His Presence flows from you to those around you.

You are His hands, His feet, His smile, His hug, and His voice in this world.

## A *"Tough Guy" Is Reduced to Tears*

After I had preached at a meeting in New York not long ago, I began to pray for people. I had noticed that three apparent gang members had come in from the streets. One look at them and I realized they were rough, tough, and angry!

Their goal, I'm sure, was to mock me and have "a little fun" at my expense. As I was praying for folks, I heard these young men calling from the back of the auditorium; then I noticed that one of them was heading toward the front.

I decided to meet him face-to-face in front of the congregation. I don't ever like to back away from a hard situation. I just "put it on the line" most of the time. I said to myself, "The Lord will have to come through, or I will be humiliated."

Either way, though, I knew I would be content, for I know I don't ever have to prove anything to anyone. All I have is by His grace. What I don't have is usually pretty obvious anyway. As I headed in his direction, I prayed silently, "Okay, Lord, I know You want to do something, and now is a good time!"

As we approached each other, I noticed that, though it was a hot summer day, he was wearing a big knit hat, a heavy army coat, and a pair of gloves. He was walking like he owned the world.

The minute he got in front of me I put my arms around him. He must have felt uncomfortable, so he began to struggle; but I was bigger than he was, and I said, "You're the one who came to me, and I'm not letting you go!"

That is when the Spirit of Jesus rose up in my innermost being, and I began to weep for him. I kissed him on the cheek and whispered in his ear, "Jesus wants you to know that He's been waiting a long time to give you this hug."

The young man fell to the floor in tears.

A second gang member came forward and said in a defiant tone of voice, "What you got for me, Preacher? I don't need your help!"

I asked Jesus to help me reach him. When the young man came near, I grabbed his coat and began to remove it from his shoulders. Then I pulled it tight around his waist and said, "The State of New York is looking for you. They want to put you in prison, but Jesus is saying, *'I have forgiven you, and I have commuted your sentence.'*"

In response, this guy just looked at me and fell to the floor as his friend had done.

I looked around for the third gang member, but he had fled from the building!

The second young man came back to our evening meeting and reported that he had gone to a court hearing and the judge had exonerated him! Jesus reached out through me, and now He was at work in this boy's heart. He gave his life to Jesus that very night!

This is the power that lives and works within us, if we would only agree with His dream for us. This is the power that seeks an outlet to others. Jesus did not possess us just to take us to Heaven someday. He came into our lives so He could accomplish great things through us. He will have those who will let Him build the Kingdom of God through them.

He has a clear and concise plan for each individual; for me and for you. When you pray the prayer He loves to answer, He will lead you and take you places you never dreamed possible!

It is as Andrew Murray points out in his book, *God's Will: Our Dwelling Place:*

> Believer, come and listen. This prayer needs your whole heart. It needs the teaching and the indwelling of Jesus Christ in the heart to be able to pray it correctly. It calls for a heart, a will, and a life entirely given up to the Father in heaven, by His Spirit dwelling in us, to understand it properly. Let the glory of God doing His will *in* us and *through* us be met by nothing less than a will wholly given up to do His will on earth as it is done in heaven. Study how God's will is done in heaven. Yield yourself to do it even so on earth.

## You Are Working With Jesus

In John 17 Jesus prays that we would all be one in Him. Why is unity so important to Him? He prayed to the Father, *"...that the world may know that You have sent Me, and have loved them as You have loved Me"* (John 17:23).

The Christ in you and me and the Christ in all other believers wants us all to come together so the world can see Him, know Him, and experience His love. In this way the world will truly see Jesus!

The day is coming when this wonderful unity will actually come into being. That is the day when all God's people will individually and collectively shout out to our Lord with a resounding "yes" that will shake Heaven and change the world we live in. What a mighty force that spirit of agreement and unity will unleash into the world.

The enemy knows that Jesus lives within you. He knows that Jesus wants to bring us all together to show the world that He is Lord. This is why the devil whispers wrong things into our ears. He wants us to get angry with each other. He wants us to be offended, hurt, and bitter toward one another. He wants us to carry grudges to our graves.

This is where gossip, slander, and backbiting come from. These are strategies of the enemy to keep us from working together, to separate us from one another. The devil knows that if we are separated from each other, God's plans and purposes cannot be accomplished.

As a divided church, we will never have the power we need to accomplish God's purposes. Knowing this, the enemy uses our pride and our stubborn egos to keep us from the unity for which Christ prayed.

Jesus said, *"Every kingdom divided against itself is brought to desolation, and every city or house divided against itself will not stand"* (Matt. 12:25).

Many Christians meet together with their fellow believers while still being separate from them in their hearts. Physical closeness is not the important thing, but spiritual closeness will keep the enemy from bringing division among us.

When God's people are close in the spirit—one in the Spirit—the enemy cannot divide them. This is why the church Jesus is building, wherever it may be, must determine in their hearts to work together with Jesus and with one another at all times.

God's people can work together! This is proven again and again every day. When hurricane Katrina struck the U.S. coast in the Gulf of Mexico, for example, thousands of Christians came together to save lives and rebuild the devastated homes and businesses along the coast. Dozens of groups worked together in an unprecedented way to get the job done and to witness the love of God by *doing* the will of God, not just arguing about what the will of God was.

Paul writes, *"For we are God's fellow workers; you are God's field, you are God's building"* (1 Cor. 3:9).

The building God is constructing is strong and impenetrable. The forces of hell will not be able to destroy it. Peter explains this clearly: *"You also, as living stones, are being built up a spiritual house, a holy priesthood, to offer up spiritual sacrifices to God through Jesus Christ"* (1 Pet. 2:5).

This is God's plan and purpose for us, His living stones. He wants us to unite with Him and one another. Imagine what would happen in the world if all believers joined hands to walk and work together. The Church of Jesus Christ would then be a mighty force for good that no one could ever tear down, and people everywhere would realize that Jesus is the Lord.

## No Need to Pretend

You are possessed by a power that is far greater than the human mind could ever comprehend. Therefore, it's important for you to realize that there is no need to pretend to have something when He already possesses you!

Many people pretend to be religious. In so doing, they deny the almighty power of God. They pretend that Jesus lives within them, but they seemingly know very little about His inherent power that is already within them.

Just to say that Jesus lives within me changes nothing, but to let Him live through me and manifest His power through me changes everything. Thank God, we don't have to engage in pretense about anything related to our faith. The living God has chosen to live and move and have His being within us! (See Acts 17:28.)

You don't have to do anything in your own power anymore. The Lord Himself calls forth His power from the heavenly dimension to meet the needs that you and those around you face in this earthly dimension. In the process of meeting your needs, He shows Himself powerful to everyone around you. He opens opportunities for you that could have come in no other way.

God doesn't need your power or your abilities. He doesn't need your counsel or advice either. Everything He needs He brings with Him when He possesses you, including faith. It seems to me that some people think it is their faith that will change the world. This is simply not so; it is the faith of Jesus Christ that changes the world.

The best we can do is say, "Yes, Jesus, come." Then He comes with His own faith and does what needs to be done through us. We don't have the compassion and love that are necessary to change the world, but, as we yield ourselves to Him, He calls His love and compassion into action in behalf of our own needs and the needs of others.

## *"Self, Just Step Aside"*

Let's face it, without the Lord Jesus Christ within us, we can't accomplish anything of eternal value. Through Him, however, we can do all things. Remember, He said, *"Most assuredly, I say to you, he who believes in Me, the works that I do he will do also;*

*and greater works than these he will do, because I go to My Father"* (John 14:12).

To do these *"greater works,"* our self-life must die. Our egos must get out of the way. Our pride must go.

He has sent His Spirit to fill us, teach us, lead us, guide us, quicken us, and empower us. The Holy Spirit is gathering us as the living Body of Christ so that the world will be able to see Him and believe in Him.

The living Christ is looking for a people through whom He can change the world. He doesn't need our talent, because He is all-powerful. He doesn't need our imperfect love, because He is love.

There's nothing religious about agreeing with your living Lord and Father. Doing so changes everything about you—the way you live, the way you think, and the way you believe.

The Holy Spirit will teach you about Jesus and bring to your remembrance the things that He has taught. He will guide you into all truth. His goal is to show Jesus to you and love the whole world through you. He wants you to learn to hear Jesus' voice and experience His love.

He has more in mind than simply giving you everything Jesus has, for you already have everything Jesus has, because He lives within you. Paul writes, *"Blessed be the God and Father of our Lord Jesus Christ, who has blessed us with every spiritual blessing in the heavenly places in Christ"* (Eph. 1:3).

Notice that this has already happened. It's in the past tense, not in the future tense. This is not for Heaven, it is for now. We do ourselves, and the Church that Jesus is building, a great disservice when we relegate these precious things to the future, when Jesus purchased them with His blood on the cross so we can experience them all here and now. Every spiritual blessing in the heavenly places in Christ is yours already!

Imagine what would happen within the church and throughout the world if the Church of Jesus Christ really knew *who* dwells within her. When this happens, I'm sure we will hear Christians shouting "yes" all over the world.

## God Is Not a Gentleman

Our all-powerful and all-knowing God must truly be tired of being dormant within so many of His people, and I'm sure He is tired of being told what to do.

For years we've been taught that He's a "gentleman," but I don't think this concept gives us a good picture of what He's really like. Certainly He is a gentleman in the sense that He won't impose His will upon us, but He does want what He paid for, and that is you and me.

Even gentlemen expect to be paid for what they do, and God is no exception. He has a destiny for your life, and He won't stop coming to you until you open your heart with a full-fledged and wholehearted "yes" to Him. Many will often try to find solace in the thought that God will push His way into our lives. They believe that God will allow them to miss their purpose for living rather than interfere with their own life's plan. But God's plan is bigger than that. It is far more important than that. He will move in our lives; He will badger us, coax us, call us, and constrain us to get our attention. We often do not see or understand the eternal value of God's purposes. Some of us just don't get it. But He gets it because He planned it from before the foundations of the earth. He will work in us and around us with every means to get our attention and to win our hearts for Himself.

Some of you know what I mean. Some of you are on the run as you read these pages. You know that God wants you. You can sense His Holy Spirit talking to you and drawing you to Him. The most exciting day of your life will be when you simply lift your heart to Him in complete surrender to Him. At that moment you will begin to understand the heart and soul of this book. He knows that you'll find true happiness, contentment, fulfillment, and joy when you cooperate with Him in living out that dream.

Everyone wants to know that their life means something. Everyone wants to leave their mark on the earth. Everyone wants to know that the world is better because they lived. This, too, is God's plan for you. Your life *does* mean something. You are intended to change the world, your world: yourself, your community, your schools, and beyond.

All of this, as we've already pointed out, will require you to have new ears, new eyes, and a new heart—a heart that can hope things that you never thought you could hope.

He is getting ready to say some things to you that you've never heard before and He is ready to show many things to you that you've never seen or considered before.

As we conclude this chapter, let's pray together:

*"Lord, bring me Your power. Bring Your love, Your mercy, Your ability, Your favor, and anything else You want to bring. Let's go do it together; let's work together to fulfill the dream You have for me. Yes, Lord, I'm Yours. Just take me. I am through resisting You. I am through fighting Your Holy Spirit. Come in and possess me, my life, and my future."*

This may well be the most exciting moment in human history for you and the entire Body of Christ, for one more believer has prayed "yes" from the bottom of his or her heart. Hallelujah!

Jesus said, *"Come to Me, all you who labor and are heavy laden, and I will give you rest. Take My yoke upon you and learn from Me, for I am gentle and lowly in heart, and you will find rest for your souls. For My yoke is easy and My burden is light"* (Matt. 11:28-30).

## SCRIPTURE REFERENCES FOR FURTHER STUDY

John 17

John 14:26

John 14:16-17

Ephesians 3:20

Ephesians 1:3

Philippians 4:13

John 15:5

Galatians 2:20

1 Peter 2:5

1 Corinthians 3:9

Matthew 28:18

Jesus said, *"When you lift up the Son of Man, then you will know that I am He, and that I do nothing of Myself; but as My Father taught Me, I speak these things. And He who sent Me is with Me. The Father has not left Me alone, for I always do those things that please Him"* (John 8:28-29).

# CHAPTER SEVEN

# Praying "Yes" for Others

Jesus, through His personal obedience to the Father, always showed us the importance of living in the will of God, and He demonstrated how such a lifestyle leads to the fulfillment of our destiny as children of God.

Thus far, we have been focusing on personal prayer, but the same principles, rooted and grounded in the will and Word of God, apply to praying for others, as well. Interceding for others as we have prayed for ourselves is a natural outgrowth of our submission to the Father's will.

Just as you want God's dream for you to come to pass, you want His dream for those you care about to come to pass too. You want to be involved in the fulfillment of His destiny for you, and by praying for others you become involved in the fulfillment of His destiny for your friends and family.

You want your life to be yielded to God in all aspects so you will not miss even the smallest detail He has planned for you. The greatest joy in life comes from knowing that you are doing exactly what you were born to do. As you step forth into the realization of this joy, God will lead you from adventure to adventure, strength to strength, joy to joy, and glory to glory.

I'm sure you want this same experience for all those you love. Through intercessory prayer you can help to make this happen for them.

## *Agreeing With God's Plan for Others*

In your prayers for others, be sure to pray for God's will to be accomplished in their lives. Open your heart to the widest range of possibilities for them that you can envision and imagine. Don't limit God by thinking fleshy limitations and leaning on your own insights. Don't limit Him by your own ideas and opinions either. Remember, God's will is usually one step beyond our natural mind. It is just over the edge of the things I am already willing to think and accept. When we are unwilling to think or go beyond these areas of emotional safety, we will miss the point, and our prayers simply cloud the spiritual atmosphere with fleshy stubbornness and unbelief. This kind of praying will do more harm than it does good. He already knows the best course of action. He already has the solution. He only needs us to agree with Him and invite His Holy Spirit to do the Father's bidding.

He is able to do far more abundantly beyond all that we ask or think, according to the power that works within us. (See Ephesians 3:20.) I don't know about you, but I can imagine quite a bit. To think that He can do far more than that opens wonderful doors of limitless possibilities.

So pray for others by asking God to do whatever He needs to do to see His dreams for their lives fulfilled. Never forget that He can open any door, grant favor, build relationships, and move miraculously in any way He chooses to accomplish His goals and aspirations in a person's life.

I will often sense that there is something God wants me to pray for, but He does not always tell me what that might be. When this happens, I simply pray in obedience to what I know, and I always try to follow the inner sense I have about the matter.

My wife, Cathy, is a seasoned and powerful intercessor. Actually, it is easy to get jealous at the way the Lord uses her so mightily in prayer. Her confidence level is so high that she often prays intensely without even knowing what the particular need may be.

During the spring of 2001, she and many, many other intercessors around the world were drawn into an intense and prolonged period of intercessory prayer. It was all-consuming for her, and her drive to pray was so strong that it could be sensed throughout our home. The Holy Spirit literally consumed her in prayer.

As spring turned into summer and summer approached autumn, the brooding of the Holy Spirit increased in its intensity, and it was so strong that Cathy could hardly continue working. This was highly unusual, for Cathy is an extremely hard worker, and many years ago she learned how to work and pray at the same time. But this was different. This intercession was just overwhelming. As I watched her over these months, I wondered what was about to happen.

As a seasoned intercessor, I have come to respect and trust the Holy Spirit within her as she responds to the Lord's leading in her "hidden" ministry of prayer. God reveals many things to her as she constantly seeks His face and His will.

As September of that year began, the intensity of her intercession was overwhelming to the extent that it spilled over to me, and I was moved to pray with her. Like her, I became very preoccupied with the need to engage in intercessory prayer.

Veteran intercessors like Cathy know how to handle such seasons of prayer, but I was a bit of a novice at it, so I asked her for information and help as I went along. I even probed her for information about what we were praying for and why we were praying.

She assured me that she didn't really know, but she was sure it was from the Lord. All she knew was that something quite incredible was about to happen. Since we had no idea what it was, we speculated that God was preparing the United States for a spiritual revival and His church for a return of His Presence.

The evening of September 10, 2001, is an evening I will remember for the rest of my life. As I was preparing for bed, still praying with all my heart and groaning in the Spirit, the intensity began to fade away. In fact, it stopped. It was gone. I no longer felt the need to pray. Then I heard these words: *"It is finished."*

I ran downstairs to find Cathy sitting in the living room with a bundle of new drapes in her arms. I blurted out, "Cathy, it's over! It's completed!"

She looked up at me and simply responded, "I know. Now all we can do is wait."

An eerie silence fell upon us. We checked our e-mail and discovered that other intercessors around the world were reporting the same experience.

No one knew what was about to happen, but the next morning, September 11, 2001, revealed why we had all been praying so fervently for so many months, as we watched the World Trade Center and the Pentagon being attacked by terrorists.

I am firmly convinced that the prayer that believers all over the world had given themselves to—the intercessory prayer of agreement with God's will—had saved us from things that could have been even more devastating and tragic than they were.

We may never know for sure all the results of that season of intercession, but we know that God allowed us to join Him in an intercessory event that would go down in history as the beginning of the war on terror around the world.

Our involvement in this was simple and unquestioning. God moved upon His people and some entered into agreement with Him even though they did not know for sure what they were praying for. The loss of life and property would have been much more severe than it was if God's intercessors had not "stood in the gap" and prayed in agreement with His will, as He was leading them to do. He had called intercessors around the world to pray and they simply said "yes" to Him.

God explained the importance of intercession to Ezekiel when He said, *"So I sought for a man among them who would make a wall, and stand in the gap before Me on behalf of the land, that I should not destroy it; but I found no one"* (Ezek. 22:30).

Thank God there were those who helped to make a wall and stand in the gap before Him in behalf of the land.

In the same way that the band of intercessors stood with God in Ezekiel's day, and intercessors prayed before 9/11, you can agree with God in prayer for those around us and those who we feel led to pray for. This is true especially when we do not know His will or do not like what we know His will is.

Additionally, God will often tell intercessors what a time of prayer is all about, but God is not a gossip, so what He shares is usually not for public announcement or prayer meeting discussion. Many a spiritual secret has been passed on from prayer meeting to prayer meeting when God intended a certain thing for your heart only. When you learn to keep intercession confidential and your prayer hidden, you will be far more useable and effective for the purposes of God. Gossip, by any other name, is still gossip!

## *"Yes" People Change the World*

Commit yourself to agree with God's plan for those you pray for. Such a commitment will require an investment of time and energy and may even be arduous at times. It is common to want good results without much effort, work, or pain, but many times the path to good results is paved with hard work and even a degree of suffering.

Part of the work may be the need to educate and help the person you are praying for. Often, this is hard work indeed, and many may shrink from it because it requires a depth of commitment and relationship that may be difficult to maintain, but it is necessary.

The Bible says, *"Bear one another's burdens, and so fulfill the law of Christ"* (Gal. 6:2). Christ's supreme law is love, and love is a vital part of your intercession for others.

When the road seems long and difficult, many get tired of the journey and they may even begin to resist God's will. Wanting immediate results, they begin to waver and they become engaged in doubting. We must never forget that the path we're on leads to the fulfillment of God's destiny in our own lives as well as the lives of others. Our faithfulness to Him will lead to fullness of joy.

## *The Most Precious Gift to Mankind*

Many wonder why God doesn't just snap His fingers and bring about the necessary changes almost instantaneously. They may ask, "Why, if God loves us so much, do we have to go through the valley of the shadow of death?" There is a simple answer to this question, but it is not pleasing to our fleshy self-life.

God has given us the most precious possession imaginable: a free will. Unlike satan, who lies, steals, and tortures people into mindless submission to his evil ways, God wants us to love Him freely, to use our free will to choose to love Him and follow Him.

He is looking for people who will choose to follow Him because they have determined that there is nothing more exciting and fulfilling than following Him and His ways. This is true love, true relationship, true harmony, and true union with God.

These are the "yes people" God is looking for, and these are the people who will change the world. The person who voluntarily agrees with God, as a matter of willful desire, will find himself

pleasing the Lord. The ones who freely love God and freely submit to Him will most certainly change the world.

This is what is needed today: people who will submit their
lives to God and His will. These folk are the salt of the earth and
the light of the world. They will make others thirsty and hungry
for God. They will lead others to taste and see how good God is.
Their light will shine in a world of darkness. They will truly
change the world.

## Obeying the Lord

Many think that obedience to God consists of simply obeying the Ten Commandments. We have been led to believe that
everything God wants us to know is written in the Bible and certain Christian books. The prevailing thought is that if we simply
do what we are told, we will please God and He will leave us
alone. But that kind of thinking goes against the fundamental
reason why we were created.

God never wanted us to be mindless slaves or fear-filled ser-
vants who only follow Him in order to stay out of hell or avoid
trouble. He has planned an awesome, unequaled life of adventure
and accomplishment for us. But all this is for those who will
cooperate with Him, people who want to allow Him to live His
life through them.

Very often, God's will is contrary to our own personal
desires. For this reason many find it hard to agree with Him and
say "yes" to His dream for their lives. This is ironic in light of the
fact that many of us will say that His ways and His thoughts are
higher and better than our own. In spite of this, we may fight
Him when we have to make the choice to allow Him to do what
He wants to do in our behalf.

A friend of mine was an avowed celibate. He was certain
that God had called him to remain single so he could serve the
Lord more fully. It seemed scriptural to him in light of some of

Paul's teachings and the examples of certain Bible characters who never got married.

Though I didn't think this was really God's will for my friend, I didn't say anything to him about it. I encouraged him when we got together to pray and seek the Lord.

I remember some of his prayers. "Lord, I am so glad You called me to be single. I happily submit to Your will and look forward to all the ways I can serve You without a wife and family. I yield to You, Lord."

It was hard for me to remain quiet when I heard him pray like that week after week. To me, it seemed as if he was using the prayer to try to convince himself that God had called him to this particular lifestyle.

One day, though, something remarkable happened. As we prayed together, he began with his usual remarks and reminders to the Lord. Then he did something that he usually did not do. He began to pray softly in tongues.

As he prayed in tongues, I received the interpretation to his prayer, which I proceeded to share with him: "Lord, I need a woman! I need a wife and family! Lord, I am so lonely! Please send me a wife!"

He was stunned, for the interpretation was a prayer that he was not ready to pray aloud. Although he never spoke of a change of heart in this regard, after a while, he found himself agreeing with this prayer, which he was able to receive as God's will for his life. Now he is happily married with four children!

## Prayers On; Hands Off!

As you can see, praying for others is as simple as praying for yourself when you learn to pray God's will for them. When we don't know His will, we pray for them anyhow, sometimes in deep intercession that is based on Jesus' words: "Not our will, not their will, but Your will be done, O Lord!"

This is not always as easy as it might seem to be. Too often, as we discussed earlier, we "pollute" the spiritual atmosphere with "stuff" from our own wills and personal desires even though we know that the best plans for us come from on high.

A few years ago my fourth son, Joel, decided that he wanted to attend Oxford University, just north of London. This was not our first choice of a college for him, however.

We are a close-knit family, and our Italian roots give us the tendency to want everyone close at home—forever! Joel's desire to go to Oxford created a difficult dilemma for Cathy and me.

How could I pray most effectively in this situation? How could I offer it to the Lord? Deep inside, I wanted to rant and rave. I felt like complaining. I wanted to beg God not to let this happen to us.

Sure, we do have four other sons, and they were in our area, but a son is a son! It took me several days of internal struggling before I could pray at all. Was I truly ready to pray the prayer I had preached all over the world? Was I going to "foul up" the spiritual air with my fleshy complaints that might even cause resistance to God's plan for Joel and His plan for us as a family?

Finally, I mustered up the strength to pray. I offered Joel and His plans to the Lord with a somewhat open mind and a semi-willing heart. In the process, however, I gave the Lord some advice as to how I thought He should respond.

At one time I would have gone much further by explaining my position to the Lord and letting Him know that it couldn't possibly be in Joel's best interests to attend Oxford. Four years in England, I would have told Him, is way too long for our son to be away from us.

As humans, we so easily forget that God already knows everything there is to know about every situation we face. He knows the situation frontward and backward. He never needs our counsel or advice. He just needs us to be willing to let Him be God in our lives.

Deep inside, I had a good feeling after I prayed. I had given the situation and Joel to the Lord, and I vowed not to allow myself to worry about it any longer. Worry is always a danger signal, a sure sign that we have not surrendered something to the Lord. Furthermore, worry always pollutes the atmosphere and confuses our wills with the dream God has for us.

After my prayer about this, I decided to take Joel with me on my next trip to London so we could spend some time touring the campus of Oxford University and speaking to the admission department. As we drove around the quaint town of Oxford and toured the campus, I did my best to encourage my son to pursue his dreams.

As God would have it, only a few moments after leaving Oxford, on our return trip to London, Joel told me that he was no longer interested in Oxford! I breathed a sigh of relief and prayed a silent "thank You" to Jesus.

I had said "yes" to God, and He responded by softening my heart so I would be able to accept what He wanted me and Joel to do. Had I insisted that Joel stay in the United States for his higher education, I might never have known God's true plan for his life. By keeping my hands off the situation, God had the freedom to work in our family in a wonderful way that assured each of us that He is fulfilling His dream for us as individuals and as a family.

In this type of approach to praying, we take our hands off and let God put His hands on the situation. I refuse to counter God's will with my earthly "wisdom." I refuse to counter His dream with my own human analysis of someone else's life, even if that "someone else" is a member of my own family.

Believe me, I do not say this lightly. I have five sons. Three of my sons are married, and I now have five grandchildren. While it is true that I am full of advice, opinions, and counsel for each of them, when I talk to them I realize that my opinions about what they should do must not enter the picture. Counsel received and appreciated is truly counsel that is asked for; otherwise it is bitter indeed!

He is their heavenly Father, and He sees them, loves them, and has created a plan for each one of them that I am only able to see in part. I know that I must not and cannot counsel the Counselor. I cannot advise the Advisor, and I cannot guide the Creator. I must come to a place where I trust the Holy Spirit to give them guidance and instruction, as He has faithfully done for all of these years.

As I write, I am reminded of one of Job's conversations with God. Please read the following words of Scripture prayerfully and carefully.

> *"Shall the one who contends with the Almighty correct Him? He who rebukes God, let him answer it."*
>
> *Then Job answered the Lord and said: "Behold, I am vile; what shall I answer You? I lay my hand over my mouth. Once I have spoken, but I will not answer; yes, twice, but I will proceed no further"*
>
> *Then the Lord answered Job out of the whirlwind, and said: "Now prepare yourself like a man; I will question you, and you shall answer Me: Would you indeed annul My judgment? Would you condemn Me that you may be justified? Have you an arm like God? Or can you thunder with a voice like His?" (Job 40:2-9).*

How many times have we polluted the spiritual air around us by begging God to do things for us? We do not understand the power of our words or our thoughts. We must remember these words from the Bible: *"For as he thinks in his heart, so is he"* (Prov. 23:7).

We often don't understand that when we lift up our own desires and will against His, we pollute the spiritual atmosphere with the sweaty and fleshy desires of mortal man. When we raise our own will in opposition to God's perfect plan for our lives and the lives of others, we are interfering with what He wants to accomplish.

We must learn to pray in harmony with God's desire for others. When we don't know His will, we should not attempt to figure out what the best solution will be and pray accordingly. We must not rely on mere human wisdom or even religious doctrines or theology. Never forget that God does not limit Himself to our flawed understanding of Himself, nor does He consign Himself to the religious boundaries imposed by denominations and churches.

We must, as faithfully as we can, listen for the voice of the Lord in whatever way He speaks to us before we even open our mouths. Once you have heard from Him, your heart will break and your spirit will leap in confident intercession before His throne of grace. Otherwise, our prayer in the Spirit has the power to move mountains, when we pray with hearts filled with faith.

All the angels of Heaven are awaiting His command to bring about His dream for each human being He has created. No amount of begging, claiming, shouting, or demanding will help, for these are the last efforts of a frustrated human spirit that is not getting its own way. These antics may make us feel better in some ways, but they do nothing to move the Lord, whose single-eyed desire is to unfold His glory to its fullest extent in our lives and the lives of those for whom we pray.

*"Call to Me, and I will answer you, and show you great and mighty things, which you do not know"* (Jeremiah 33:3).

## SCRIPTURE REFERENCES FOR FURTHER STUDY

James 5:16

Matthew 6:6

Luke 11:1

Jeremiah 33:3

1 Thessalonians 5:16-18

Luke 18:1

Romans 8:26

Acts 6:4

Romans 12:12

Philippians 4:6

The Christian author George McDonald writes, *"There is a communion with God that asks for nothing, yet asks for everything...He who seeks the Father more than anything He can give, is likely to have what he asks, for he is not likely to ask amiss."*

# CHAPTER EIGHT

# The Password
and the Portal

As mentioned previously, the password that enables you to enter into this wonderful communion with God is "yes," for "yes" asks for nothing and for everything at the same time. The "everything of God" is what we receive when we say "yes" to Him.

As you begin each new day, review the blessings God has showered upon you and reflect upon His power in your life as the following affirmations declare:

Yes, God, I know You have a dream for me and I want You to have Your way in my life (see Matt. 26:39).

Yes, God, I know You will supply all my need according to Your riches in glory by Christ Jesus (see Phil. 4:19).

Yes, God, I know I can do all things through Christ who strengthens me (see Phil. 4:13).

Yes, God, I know I am more than a conqueror through Him who loves me (see Rom. 8:37).

Yes, God, I know that all things are mine in Christ (see 1 Cor. 3:21).

Yes, God, I know I belong to Christ, and He belongs to You (see 1 Cor. 3:23).

Yes, God, I know that all things have become new in my life (see 2 Cor. 5:17).

Yes, God, Your abounding grace is always with me (see 2 Cor. 9:8).

Yes, God, You daily load me with benefits (see Ps. 68:19).

You see, your "yes" to God opens the door to close and abiding fellowship with Him in which you find everything you need.

It truly is the password into the Kingdom of God and into His throne room, where you will enjoy sweet communion with Him every day of your life.

"But how can a simple, one-word prayer offer so much?" you may ask. Well, you are certainly not the first person to ask such a question. Remember that your "yes" to God is a heartfelt, heart-meant prayer that, in its utterance, yields your heart, your soul, and your dreams to Him. By praying in this way you are trusting and believing Him that the best you can experience in this whole world comes when you let God have His way in your life.

It is a prayer of abandonment and surrender to the One who created you, loves you, and always wants the best for you.

## *The Portal Is You!*

The password is "yes," and the portal is you! There is a living, dynamic relationship that God wants to have with you, and it's not just a weekly visit on Sunday mornings. It's a moment-by-moment, day-by-day, life-giving fellowship that develops as you learn to abide in His will and His Manifest Presence.

By saying that the portal between the earthly dimension and the heavenly dimension is you, I mean that everything mentioned above and everything that is mentioned in the Scriptures are yours already through Jesus Christ, and by agreeing with

God, you enable everything that is in eternity to pour through you and out to others.

All the promises of God are "yes" and "amen" in Jesus, and He lives within you. (See Second Corinthians 1:20.) In the Most Holy Place of God's Presence you can continuously enjoy everything He has for you. He truly is the Giver of every good and perfect gift. (See James 1:17.) He is your loving heavenly Father who has great and wonderful things in store for you right now.

In the Presence of God you don't have to struggle and strive any longer. You don't have to pretend to act like Jesus anymore. You don't even have to ask, "What would Jesus do?", for what He would do is far greater than anything we can come up with even in our wildest imagination. You simply say "yes" to Him and then you rest in Him. You let Him live His life through you, and He will do what needs to be done.

Jesus will show Himself to the world through you, if you will let Him. You are a portal through which He wants to flow. People will know there is a living, exalted Christ living in you, because they will see His love and power in your life flowing like a river through you.

In the same way that Jesus is the doorway to a whole new way of life for you, you can be the doorway through which He brings His power to the world.

## *The Presence of God*

Contrary to some modern thought, we can practice, that is *experience*, the Presence of God on a continuous basis. This is possible because Jesus has washed us with His Blood that never loses its power and never loses its purpose. His Blood is a continuous pathway into His Presence. We cannot worship our way into His Presence. We cannot pray our way there or fast our way there, for entrance into His Presence is a *gift* of God's love and grace.

Abiding there is a gift from our Father as well. He wants us to live with Him in His Presence, so He made a way for this to happen. But we are so often distracted by the worries, the lusts, and the personal struggles of life that we cannot experience what we have, who we are, and where we are in Him!

The enemy of your soul wants you to be self-centered, desiring your own needs to be met first, thinking about your own problems, and concentrating on your own troubles. This is what the enemy will trick you into thinking. The problem is that worry will never bring the peace of God. Self-centeredness in any form will never allow you to experience the Presence of God.

As you have probably guessed, God has much better pastimes for you than worry! His plan is very different from anything the world has to offer.

God says, *"Be anxious for nothing, but in everything by prayer and supplication, with thanksgiving, let your requests be made known to God; and the peace of God, which surpasses all understanding, will guard your hearts and minds through Christ Jesus"* (Phil. 4:6-7).

In the Presence of God there is peace—a peace that surpasses all understanding. Even in the midst of great trauma, there is an assurance of His plan because of His Presence. There is no worry or anxiety there whatsoever, because God's perfect love casts out all fear. (See First John 4:18.)

The enemy of your soul wants you to believe that there is no hope and no help for you or for the problems of the world. If you choose to believe that there is no hope, you will become hopeless, and you will not look up to the true Source of all your hope and help. Your help comes from the Lord—the One who made Heaven and the earth.

God manifested Himself through His Son, Jesus, in order to demonstrate the power of the heavenly dimension to us. Jesus was a portal through which He manifested Himself to hopeless and helpless people everywhere. God brought hope to the world through His Son.

It was as if He said, *"I am going to send My Son to the earth, and for three years I am going to show humanity what can happen when humanity submits to Me."*

Those were three awesome and incredible years! Really, they were the most wonderful three years in all human history, for during those three years Jesus demonstrated the power of another dimension on this earth. During that period of 1,095 days, amazing things happened wherever He went.

Jesus was filled with power, love, and compassion! He healed the sick, raised the dead, and rebuked the religious, turning the religious system on its head. He performed innumerable miracles, spoke outstanding truths, manifested God's power, and opened the gates of Heaven to us!

His was more than an extraordinary life; it was an extraterrestrial life that was endued with power and authority that the world had never seen before. Recognizing this in Him, people followed Him by the thousands.

They followed Him, and He revealed to them immense power, the power of the dimension from which He came, omnipotent power. Many people, though, could not handle such power being in their midst, so they crucified Him.

Jesus responded to their false accusations, persecution, and the ultimate death sentence with the words that shall ever be the standard for our lives. He said to the Father, *"...nevertheless, not as I will, but as You will"* (Matt. 26:39). This was always the theme of Jesus' life.

He explained to His disciples what would happen after His death by telling them that He was about to return to His Father in Heaven, but that He would send His Spirit to be with us and in us.

He didn't want the hearts of His disciples to be troubled. Nonetheless, one of his disciples, Philip, remained confused, and He asked Jesus to show them the Father so he could stop worrying about what would happen in the future.

Jesus explained, *"Have I been with you so long, and yet you have not known Me, Philip? He who has seen Me has seen the Father; so how can you say, 'Show us the Father?' Do you not believe that I am in the Father, and the Father in Me? The words that I speak to you I do not speak on My own authority; but the Father who dwells in Me does the works"* (John 14:9-10).

It was then that Jesus issued an astounding promise that still holds true for all of us. He said, *"Most assuredly, I say to you, he who believes in Me, the works that I do he will do also; and greater works than these he will do, because I go to My Father"* (John 14:12).

## Demonstrating the Power of Another Dimension

In effect, Jesus had prophesied, *"Now, this is what is going to happen to Me and you. I'm going to My Father, but eventually I will come back. In the meantime, I'm sending My Sprit to be with you, love you, empower you, and guide you."*

This means that the power of another dimension—the Kingdom of God—will be within us and ready to flow through us as we yield to Him. Jesus went on to explain that we will be able to do the very things He did when He walked the earth, and we will be able to do even greater things than those!

He had demonstrated the power of God in the midst of the people time after time. Truly, the half has never yet been told of all He did during the three years He ministered on earth. Again, however, we must remember that Jesus told us often that He only did the things He saw His Father in Heaven doing. What a secret! Watch what God is doing and do it with Him! Find out what He wants to do, and do it! See what is on His heart and say "yes" to it. Agree with Him.

Now His Spirit—the Holy Ghost—lives within you, and because this is true, unlimited potential and possibility is yours!

This is how the Lord changes the world—through you, as you say "yes" to Him. In this way you will learn to say His words and touch people with His hands. You will hug people, and God's love and warmth will flow through you to them.

People will notice that there is something different about you. Some will even ask you, "What is this 'thing' that you have?" When this happens you will be able to point them to the living Christ, the One who lives within you by His Spirit. The light of God's presence will shine through you, and you will be able to lead them to Him who is the way, the truth, and the life. (See John 14:6.)

Absolute surrender to the Lord of your life is necessary for these things to be accomplished in you and through you. In his book entitled *Absolute Surrender*, Andrew Murray writes:

> When I speak of full surrender, I am not speaking about the surrender of our sins, though it may be that you need to do that: perhaps a violent temper, a bad habit, sins that have never been given up for the sake of your relationship with Christ. I am afraid that unconsciously many compromise, having the idea that they cannot be without sin; that we all must sin every day; we cannot help it. But our cry to God should be: "Lord, keep me from sin!" Surrender is about yielding yourself completely to Jesus. He will speak to you about any sin that you are not aware of.

## The Life of Jesus Christ

God is looking for people who will be willing to surrender their lives completely to Jesus Christ so they will be able to demonstrate His life to the world. Jesus is the Head of the Church, and He wants His people to do what He directs them to do.

When the Church of Jesus Christ learns how to demonstrate His life to the world, everything will change, for He will be able to do what He wants to do through His people—the portals through whom He manifests His Presence to the world.

The Holy Spirit is brooding over the church, and He is brooding over you. Indeed, He is groaning over you, awaiting your response to Him.

The near future is going to be a time of testing and trial, but it will also be a time of great glory and blessing in the lives of Christians who have learned to say "yes" to God. Ordinary people will be greatly used to do extraordinary things. He will use what the world calls "common people" to preach His Word and live His Word around the world.

These are the people Peter writes about in his epistle: *"But you are a chosen generation, a royal priesthood, a holy nation, His own special people"* (1 Pet. 2:9).

We are the special people God has chosen and called to do His work on this earth during this time. The King James Version calls us "a peculiar people." And truly we are peculiar (different and unusual) because we've said "yes" to our heavenly Father.

Every believer will have to decide what they will do. Either they will agree with God or they will sit and watch what He will do. Most of those who will not agree with His plan for them will sit in the seat of the scornful, shaking a "religious finger" in judgment and condemnation of others, as God does His marvelous things through those who learn to flow with Him.

I don't want to be sitting, watching, or shaking my finger; I want to be in the middle of the marvelous things God is doing and will do. I want to be involved in making those spectacular things happen.

It is a true statement that the simple "yes" agreement with God will launch those who pray it from their heart onto an exciting and life-changing journey that will change the world.

## A Lamp for God's Anointing

You have the opportunity to be a lamp for the Lord's anointing. Jesus said, *"You are the light of the world"* (Matt. 5:14). He is saying to you right now, *"Let there be light"*—in you. These are the very words He spoke as He created the universe.

Let there be light in your life, and let it shine forth all over the world. Let His light dispel the darkness within you and around you. As you allow His Presence to grow within you and you enjoy blessed fellowship with Him, His light will shine brightly through your eyes, your smile, your words, and your actions. You will truly be the light of the world.

As moths are attracted to the warmth and brightness of street lights on a summer's eve, people will be attracted to you as you reflect the light of God's love and Presence in our dark and dying world. They will look to you for the answers they seek.

A lamp serves a variety of purposes. It banishes the darkness, it guides us through the darkness, it serves as a beacon of warning and hope to others, it brightens our lives, it has the power to purify and cleanse, and it radiates warmth. As a lamp of the Lord's Presence and anointing, you can serve each of these purposes wherever you are.

Let's pray together with softness of heart and with a true desire to give ourselves to Him:

> *"Lord Jesus, take me to the next level. Take me where You want me to go. Take me to the city. Take me to the newspapers. Take me to television. Take me to government. Take me into the educational system. Take me to corporate America. Take me and help me start a business. Just take me and use me. Let your light shine forth through me into the darkness."*

The door is open for you to enter into the Kingdom of God and the very throne room of the Father, becoming the portal through which the light of His Kingdom will shine, bringing hope, love, and power from the heavenly dimension into this world of darkness.

*"But you are a chosen generation, a royal priesthood, a holy nation, His own special people, that you may proclaim the praises of Him who called you out of darkness into His marvelous light"* (**1 Peter 2:9**).

## SCRIPTURE REFERENCES FOR FURTHER STUDY

Isaiah 26:3

Psalm 119:105

Philippians 4:13

Philippians 4:6-7

Philippians 4:19

Matthew 5:14

1 Peter 2:9

John 14:12

John 14:6

John 14:9-10

Matthew 26:39

1 John 4:18

*"So let no one judge you in food or in drink, or regarding a festival or a new moon or sabbaths, which are a shadow of things to come, but the substance is of Christ"*
(Galatians 2:16-17).

# CHAPTER NINE

# The Shadow
# or the Substance?

Peter Pan, the main character in Sir J.M. Barrie's classic of children's literature, *Peter Pan,* lost his shadow in Wendy's bedroom, or so the story goes. He went one way, but his shadow went another way. What was he to do? What did it mean for his shadow to be disobedient to the reality that was his body? It was as though his shadow had a mind and will of its own.

This was quite a paradox for Peter Pan to have to face. After all, it is an important law of physics that a person's shadow should follow that person in precise response to what he or she does. So, this was far too much for Peter to understand or accept. He was certain that the true reality was his physical body, but then why did his shadow not follow his body as it was supposed to do? The shadow was there to give credence to what his body did. How could the body be real if the shadow did not obey it?

To have the shadow not follow the body in perfect response seemed to put in doubt the reality of Peter's own body. As the story goes, Peter Pan cried because his shadow was not in sync with his body. And why not? It is absurd for the shadow to make its own statement, to have its own reality, to do its own thing.

But Wendy had the solution to the problem. She simply sewed Peter's shadow back onto his body. The rebellion of his shadow came to an abrupt end when it was safely reattached to his body.

This simple story asks a difficult question, and it grossly fails in its attempt to resolve the problem. What happens when the shadow (our theology) fails to respond correctly to the reality of our walk with the Lord? Which is correct? Is it the responsibility of the body to respond to the shadow, no matter what it seems to say, or is it the responsibility of the shadow to obey the body?

In this instance, the laws of nature agree with the Word of God. The "shadow" of the Old Covenant was cast by the Living Christ, who is the substance of our life and faith. Christ does not respond to our theology (our shadow); He responds to the will of His Father. He moves according to the dream God has dreamed for each of us. Shadows must, by natural law and spiritual principle, follow the reality of Jesus, who alone casts a shadow.

We might tend to think of a dream as being something without substance, but God's dream for you and me is profound and substantial in every way, and His dreams become reality when we say "yes" to Him.

We might even think that the word "yes" is a little word without much substance, but one glance at a dictionary shows us that it has a deep meaning, for it expresses agreement and assent, conveying many positive things.

When we agree with God in response to His dream for us, our lives take on a new meaning and substance, a reality that they never knew before. Indeed, we can take our stand and walk upon the substance they provide for us.

The substance, the reality, is Christ. When we make a decision to go through the gate that leads from the outer court to the inner court, we are headed in the right direction, for in the inner court we see many things that point us to Christ, but these are but shadows of Him until we actually enter the Most Holy Place (the Holy of Holies)—the Manifest Presence of God.

The Most Holy Place of God's Presence is also known as "the secret place." It is a secret place only in the sense that few ever take the privilege to enter this realm. When they do so, however, they leave the shadows behind and they actually enter into Christ.

That is why so much seems to change when we enter into His Manifest Presence. We are no longer trying to figure out life by interpreting shadows. We see Him for who He really is. No more grayness, no more shadow. We see Him in the brightness of His Presence.

You should try playing the following parlor game, and you will understand clearly what I mean. Turn out all lights in the room and shine a light on the wall. Hold an object in front of the light so it casts a shadow on the wall. Then let everyone take a turn at trying to figure out what the object is by looking only at its shadow. Wow! You will then begin to understand why there are so many denominations and interpretations of the Bible! Arguments and opinions come quickly to an end when the object that created the shadow is allowed to be seen.

Jesus wants to show Himself to us clearly and directly. Check out Hebrews 10:1: *"For the law, having a shadow of the good things to come, and not the very image of the things, can never with these same sacrifices, which they offer continually year by year, make those who approach perfect."*

The reality is Jesus Himself! The shadow can only be understood when one sees the reality of Jesus. If the shadow is not responding to the reality of the living Christ, it is the shadow that needs to be "sewn" to the reality of the living Jesus, who is the reality of life itself. Simply, the reality casts the shadow and controls its shape on the wall. The shadow never takes the lead. *It always follows!*

We were never called to serve the shadow, which is open to misinterpretation, misunderstanding, and confusion. We are called to serve the living reality of the One who casts the shadow—the Light of the world, our Lord Jesus Christ.

The reality of Jesus, being alive and well in our hearts, is simple and liberating. His living reality within us helps us to see that:

In Christ there are no shadows (see James 1:17).

In Christ we find substance and meaning (see Col. 2:17).

In Christ we have redemption and forgiveness of sins (see Col. 1:14).

In Christ we have peace and confidence (see Eph. 2:14).

In Christ we have joy unspeakable and full of glory (see 1 Pet. 1:8).

In Christ, the reason we were born, the dream He has for us, begins to unfold in all its glorious fullness (see Jer. 29:11).

Jesus is the substance of life. He is our hope and our peace, and He carries in His heart the true substance of our lives.

The things of this earth, the things that so many are striving after, don't last. This is because they have no substance. Your destiny is not of the earth, for the earth is but a shadow. Your destiny is in the heart of God Himself.

## The Manifestation of the Living Christ

The things that will change the world and bring substance out of chaos are the things of Christ, which He will manifest to the world through you and me. The Holy Spirit is brooding over us to get us to understand that He wants to live His life through us. He wants to demonstrate His living Presence to the nations through us.

All we have to do is relinquish control of our lives to Him and He will do it.

In *The Way to God,* the well-known evangelist D.L. Moody writes:

> Christ is not only our way. He is the light on the way. He says, "I am the light of the world" (John 8:12; 9:5; 12:46). He goes on to say, "He that followeth Me shall not walk in darkness, but shall have the light of life" (John 8:12). It is impossible for any man or woman who is following Christ to walk in darkness. If your soul is in darkness, groping around in the fog and mist of earth, it is because you have gotten away from the true light. Nothing but light will dispel darkness....He is the Sun of Righteousness. It is our privilege to walk in the light of an unclouded sun.

## A "Secret" of the Most Holy Place

In the Most Holy Place we experience things we've never experienced before. We hear things we've never heard before. We see things we've never seen before. It's an exciting place to be, because it is where God is. This is how we begin to do things that have never been done before. For His Presence is the place of revelation, understanding, protection, and power where one is released to go forth in strength, love, faith, and truth.

Truth is dimensional in the sense that the truths you live by emanate from the dimension in which you choose to live. Fish live and breathe under water, but if you take a fish out of that dimension, it will die.

By the same token, we breathe oxygen-rich air in our earthly environment, but if we jump into the water and try to breathe underwater, we will drown. This happens because the rules of that dimension (the habitat of water) are different from the rules on land.

But the natural realm gives us insights into the spiritual dimension. Oftentimes we can learn how the spiritual realm works by observing the natural. The philosopher might say, "As on earth, so in Heaven."

The Bible tells us that "the latter rain" is the Holy Spirit being poured forth from Heaven. So we have "the former rain" and "the latter rain" available to us. The former rain found a place within us earlier in our lives, and it became the river of God, which is always full of water (the water of life). We should make sure that His river within us keeps on flowing and is never dammed or blocked by anything that should not be there.

This will ensure that we will be ready for "the latter rain" when it falls from Heaven and produces a double portion of the Holy Spirit that is so powerful that it will literally turn the world upside down. The time of the "former rain" and the "latter rain" is now. It has been so since the Day of Pentecost described in Acts 2.

The "double portion" is always available to us as a result of the Cross of Jesus. He bought it for us. Always draw from His River within you and always be open to His "spiritual rain" from Heaven, for then you will live in the double portion of His Spirit no matter where you work or where He sends you.

This promise is a true secret of the Most Holy Place, a secret with great substance for each of us and a part of God's great dream for all of His people.

Your job is to keep the river flowing, for the river is the veritable Presence of God. It is His Presence stirring deep within you and wanting to flow out through you.

You can experience His Presence 24 hours a day, 7 days a week. It doesn't matter what you feel. Let the Presence of God spring up like a well within you, and keep the channels open and unclogged so this mighty river will always be able to flow freely.

On a recent trip to Europe, as we were driving through some parts of southern Italy, the fact that it was the dry season there became apparent to all of us, for most of the vegetation we saw was brown and parched. Once in a while, though, we came to spots where the acreage was plush and green, and the grape arbors in these places were loaded with big, juicy grapes.

I noticed that the villas on these properties were awesome, and their owners' automobiles were very nice, as well. Flowers were growing everywhere around their homes and in their gardens.

The contrast between these homes and properties and the homes of the people who lived where the land was dry and parched was obvious. It seemed as if the latter folks were barely surviving.

I made mention of this to my host, the driver, by saying, "It's really lucky for the guys who have water on their property, isn't it?"

He said, "Oh, but you don't understand, there is water underneath this land everywhere. The people who have the arbors are the ones who were willing to pay the price to dig the wells. But there is water under the whole countryside."

I discovered that the ones with the fruitful arbors and beautiful flowers were the ones who realized the river was under the ground. They had tapped into the river of life, and because they did so, they were able to enjoy the bounty of nature.

The spiritual counterpart to this is clear. The well of God's Presence is within you, and it will spring up and flow out through you to give the water of life to thirsty people everywhere. By now you know how this will happen; you must agree with God's will by praying the prayer He loves to answer each day of your life.

There is a chorus that shares this truth in a powerful way:

Spring up, O well, within my soul,

Spring up, O well, and overflow.

Spring up, O well, flow out through me,

Spring up, O well, set others free.

## *Our War Is Really Over*

No one can build when they are fighting. The war must end before any meaningful building can occur. Your "yes" to God releases all His power to fulfill His dream for you, but it also allows Him to do battle for you. You cannot possibly outwit, out-argue, or out-fight the enemy, but your Lord has done so and always will do so. When you let Him do the fighting, you can concentrate on the building.

Your war is over. Isaiah wrote, *"Comfort, yes, comfort My people!"* (Isa. 40:1). These were God's words being spoken through the prophet. He continued, *"Speak comfort to Jerusalem, and cry out to her, that her warfare is ended..."* (Isa. 40:2).

There is great comfort in knowing that our warfare has ended. When you begin to understand the power of the river of God within you, you will know that you don't have to fight the devil anymore. Instead, you will enjoy the peace and comfort that come from dwelling in the river and basking in the Presence of God's light and love.

God wants everything about you to change, not just your thoughts, but everything. "Change" is not a bad word, nor is it a matter of legalism. We don't change ourselves in order to get into Heaven; we change so we can hear the voice of the Lord and experience His wonderful Presence and do all the incredible things He has planned for us to do, now, in this life, at a young enough age that we can make a difference in the world.

Let Him change you from within. Let His mighty river flush out all the dross and replace it with His holiness, righteousness, and purity. This is hydropower of the strongest sort.

## Moving From the "Maybe" to the "Yes"

"Yes" is the bridge between this dimension and the Presence of God. When we enter the "yes" of God, there are no more "maybes." We need to decide, once and for all time, to move from the realm of "maybe" and truly enter the "yes" of God. This chases away the shadows and gives substance and meaning to our lives. In the Most Holy Place you will hear God speaking to you. When that happens, your only response will be, "Yes!"

More than 20 years ago, as I mentioned in Chapter 1, the Lord called me to begin a publishing ministry. I knew the verse that says that of the making of books there is no end (see Eccles. 12:12), so I questioned the Lord by saying, "Why write another book?"

His response to me was a real surprise. He said, *"Why write another song?"* He showed me that songs and books not only chronicle our journey through this dimension of time, but that we need new books and new songs all the time through which the Lord can speak new things to His people both in this generation and the generations not yet born.

God wanted me to publish the prophets, and prophets always have a new word from God for us.

For more than two decades it has been my privilege to do so. I knew the call of God was on my life and, as a result, I knew there could be no more "maybes" or shadows in my life. I had to say "yes" to Him, and I'm so glad I did, and I am happy and content that I still do...most of the time! It gives my life a new sense of purpose, mission, and direction.

## *"Here I Am, Lord, Use Me"*

On a ministry trip I felt led of the Lord to preach the same message for 15 meetings in a row. My topic was "Living in the 'Yes' of God." It was a most incredible experience.

By the end of that week a new song came forth. It said, in part, "I say 'yes.' I say 'yes' to Your Presence and say 'yes' to Your love."

It was a perfect "yes" and "amen" to the services, because the musician was echoing the Word that had been shared. As the meetings concluded, therefore, we all walked forward with a new understanding of the Word, an understanding that we sang back to God in worship.

I thank Him for the songs He gives to His people. Many of these songs are prophetic messages from His heart. For example, we need to agree with the song that says, "Every move I make I make in You [Jesus]. You make me move, Jesus." These lines point us to the One who lives within us, the One who wants to direct and control our lives. They show us that we live, and move, and have our being in Him. (See Acts 17:28.)

The Lord sees everything from the vantage point that is provided by another dimension—the dimension in which He resides. He works from that dimension, and so should we. The more we see things as He sees them and then trust Him in those areas, the more we will simply keep quiet before Him and do what He tells us to do. This will help us to agree with Him at all times. We will respond to Him by saying, "Here I am, Lord, use me."

Even when things seem a little scary or murky, we can still trust that He is in control. Doing so brings us into the realm of a Jesus-centered theology instead of a self-centered philosophy. It takes us from the shadows into the substance.

As we learn to be Jesus-centered, we realize that we exist for Him alone, not for ourselves. He offers us a life to be lived for His pleasure, not our own. To know that we are used by Him in order for Him to accomplish what He wants to accomplish through us is one of life's greatest joys.

## *Where Is Your Consciousness Resting?*

Where do you rest your consciousness? The choice is a simple one: either you rest your consciousness in the Spirit (the "yes" of God), or you place it in the natural realm where there is very little rest.

By resting your consciousness in the Spirit, you are automatically in constant communion with God. If I am sitting in my office and you are not near me and want to talk with me, you will need to pick up the phone and call me. If, however, you come into my office and sit in my presence, all you have to do is talk to me face to face and person to person.

The communication is so much better when you are in my presence, because we can see each other's facial expressions, body language, and gestures—something we cannot do by phone.

It's the same with God. We can call to Him from this earthly dimension or we can enter into His dimension. This should be your goal—to move into the same "room" with Him and have fellowship with Him, for this is His desire for you.

You want to be with Him, and He wants to be with you. In His presence you will find true rest, and, you will discover the truth of what Jesus said to Mary, that having fellowship with Him is the most important thing in life. (See Luke 10:41-42.)

## *The Shadow and the Son*

The Bible says that God has *"...called you out of darkness into His marvelous light"* (1 Pet. 2:9). The darkness is the place of shadows, but in God's marvelous light, we experience the Son who is the Light of our lives and the substance of our faith.

One of the Ten Commandments tells us to remember the Sabbath day, to keep it holy. This causes many people to think that if they miss church on Sunday, they are almost damned, because they haven't kept it holy.

In the Most Holy Place (the place of God's Presence), the Sabbath is not a day, for a day is simply symbolic of a condition of life; it is the state of the heart. It is a place of rest—a rest from our own religious labors in an attempt to gain favor with God. The true Sabbath is a spiritual place of total trust in Him. Under the New Covenant, the Sabbath was never meant to be a day, for the Sabbath day had been only a shadow of what was yet to come. The substance represented by the Sabbath belongs to God and it comes completely from Him.

The subject of the tithe is another area that helps us to see the difference between shadow and substance. Many people believe that tithing is giving 10 percent, but in the Most Holy Place we learn that God expects us to be His tithe. When we live in God's Presence, we understand that He wants all of us, not just a percentage. He sends us to the nations to accomplish His will and fulfill His dream. The 10 percent was only a shadow; the substance comes when we yield to Him in full surrender.

The same thing can be said about worship. We can sing songs, we can praise God, and we can engage in worship, but in the Presence of God, our very lives become worship to the Father.

Even our breath becomes worship to the Lord. The fact that we are living, breathing creatures is anathema to the enemy, because our very existence proclaims to him and all the spirits in the universe that we are alive and God is alive in us!

It's time for all of us to move out of the shadows into the realm of life and substance. We need to put all shadows behind us and begin relating to the Substance, who is Jesus Christ, the Lord.

# What Revelation Is

Revelation is when the truth becomes so powerful, so alive, that it changes your life. If it doesn't change your life, it's not revelation; it's just something thought-provoking or interesting.

The "yes" of God is the place of revelation, where God reveals Himself and His ways to us. In the "yes" of God you realize more fully than ever before that it's all about Him, not about you. It is there that we learn to say with Paul, "I die daily," and we understand what John the Baptist meant when he said, "He must increase, but I must decrease."

These are the spiritual revelations that truly change our lives.

Jesus said, *"I have food to eat of which you do not know"* (John 4:32). He went on to explain this metaphor to His disciples: *"My food is to do the will of Him who sent Me, and to finish His work"* (John 4:34).

Jesus found His food, His satisfaction, and His fulfillment in doing His Father's will. That's where you will find those things, as well.

Shadow to substance changes everything, makes life worth living, and is always an adventure. Substance is a place of revelation from Him.

Your challenge is to move out of the shadows and find the Substance. Move out of the flesh and find spiritual peace. Move out of the earthly dimension and enjoy the Kingdom of God. Move out of the self-life and enter the life of Christ.

There's a river of life that's waiting to flow out of you.

*"Therefore we also, since we are surrounded by so great a cloud of witnesses, let us lay aside every weight, and the sin which so easily ensnares us, and let us run with endurance the race that is set before us, looking unto Jesus, the author and finisher of our faith, who for the joy that was set before Him endured the cross, despising the shame, and has sat down at the right hand of the throne of God"* (Hebrews 12:1-2).

## SCRIPTURE REFERENCES FOR FURTHER STUDY

John 4:32-34

Hebrews 11:1

1 Peter 2:9

Luke 10:42

Acts 17:28

Ecclesiastes 12:122

2 Corinthians 1:20

Isaiah 40:1-2

The prophet Jeremiah spoke forth these words from God: *"For I know the thoughts that I think toward you, says the Lord, thoughts of peace and not of evil, to give you a future and a hope. Then you will call upon Me and go and pray to Me, and I will listen to you. And you will seek Me and find Me, when you search for Me with all your heart"* (Jeremiah 29:11-13).

# CHAPTER TEN

# Points of Destiny

Success is not an accident, it is a series of right choices that result in both achieving of your goals and the unfolding of your destiny. You control both. You decide the direction of your life, your future, your destiny.

William Jennings Bryan said, "Destiny is not a matter of chance, it is a matter of choice. It is not a thing to be waited for, it is a thing to be achieved."

This is what we have been saying, that God has a plan and purpose for your life. He has dreamed a dream for you; your cooperation with Him in the unfolding and the fulfillment of His dream for you will most certainly bring it to pass. This is the choice that each of us must make every day.

Destiny, from a biblical perspective, is not a single point in time; it is not a career and it is not only a future event. Destiny is not something you arrive at, for it is unfolding all the time. Destiny unfolds in the now of your life no matter where you are, what you are doing, how you are living, or what you are feeling. Your destiny is unfolding now.

Your destiny is to know God, to hear Him, and to let Him live His life through you. In short, your destiny is to be conformed into His Image now, in this lifetime. The Christian writer Andrew Maclaren puts it well: "Get near to God if you want to enjoy what He has purposed for you. Live in simple, loving fellowship with Him if you desire to drink in His fullness....If we want to get our needs supplied, our weakness strengthened, and wisdom to dispel our perplexity, we must be where all the provisions are stored."

That place is the Presence of God.

## Hearing God

We hear the voice of God in many different ways. He speaks to us through nature, through His Word, through other believers, through circumstances, and through the "still, small voice" of His Holy Spirit. We hear Him through His inner witness, through angels, through prophets, through preachers and teachers, through Christian books, and through a multitude of other means. But, most of all, He speaks to us as we learn to have fellowship with Him, one to One, within the "yes" of God, the Most Holy Place—His Manifest Presence.

God has called us to union with Himself. Every father who loves his children wants to be with them, to spend quality time with them. As a father and grandfather, one of my life's greatest joys is spending time with my five sons, their wives, and my precious grandchildren.

Your heavenly Father loves you. He wants to spend time with you. He wants to hear your voice. The truth is, He wants to be with you more than you want to be with Him. His heart is filled with delight when you choose to spend time with Him, and He longs for you to express your love to Him. The time you spend with Him, the more you will yield to Him and more union you will experience. That is, the more you allow Him to express Himself through you to the world around you.

The Psalmist writes, *"Be still, and know that I am God"* (Ps. 46:10). Being still allows our soul to hear Him and trust Him in greater and greater levels. As we are still before Him we get to know Him, and we get to know His voice. He speaks to us and shares His heart with us, as deep calls to deep. (See Psalm 42:7.) As we listen to Him, our destiny begins to unfold to us and within us, and God reveals the deep things of His sacred mysteries to us.

Hearing God every day is a great start, but you must do more than just listen; you must agree with what He says to you. This is how the process of the fulfillment of your destiny works.

You must say "yes" to Jesus every day of your life. No wonder the Scripture says that His mercy is new every morning. (See Lamentations 3:22-23.) Every day gives new opportunity, new hope, new possibilities as we enter into agreement with His will for us.

*Today* is the beginning of eternity. Your destiny is not just something in the far distant future; it is now, it is today, and it is walked out during each present moment of your life.

James writes, *"Draw near to God and He will draw near to you"* (James 4:8). This is an inviolable principle. It always works.

Jonathan Edwards, the great Puritan preacher who was instrumental in America's Great Awakening, wrote, "The enjoyment of God is the only happiness with which our souls can be satisfied...fully to enjoy God, is infinitely better than the most pleasant accommodations...."

## A Purifying Hope

John writes, "Beloved, now we are children of God; and it has not yet been revealed what we shall be, but we know that when He is revealed, we shall be like Him, for we shall see Him as He is. And everyone who has this hope in Him purifies himself, just as He is pure" (1 John 3:2-3).

Don't ever let anything come between you and Him, between you and His wonderful purpose for your life. Jesus said,

*"But seek first the kingdom of God and His righteousness, and all these things shall be added unto you"* (Matt. 6:33).

In his powerful book entitled *Like Christ*, Andrew Murray writes these words: "Above all, remember what still remains the chief thing. It is Jesus, the living, loving Savior, who Himself enables you to be like Him in all things. His sweet fellowship, His tender love, and His heavenly power make it a blessedness and joy to be like Him, the Crucified One. They make the crucifixion life a life of resurrection-joy and power. In Him, the two are inseparably connected. In Him, you have the strength to always be singing the triumphant song: God forbid that I should glory, save in the cross of our Lord Jesus Christ, through which the world has been crucified unto me, and I unto the world."

## Dealing With Distractions

Marriage counselors will sometimes say, "The reason why many marriages fall apart is because a third person enters the picture." This "third person" in the marriage is not God, of course, but it can be another person, a job, troubled emotions, losses, fears, financial problems, and many other things. Anything that enters the picture and causes distractions and disruptions is the "third person."

This also can happen in our walk with the Lord. "Third persons" may enter the picture, causing confusion, distractions, disruptions, and insecurity. Their effect is to change our focus from fulfilling our destiny to dealing with trivia in the world.

These are schemes of the enemy that are designed to interrupt your daily fellowship with the Lord, and they must be recognized as such.

The "third person" could come in the form of a fear or a worry. It can even be religion itself, or it may take the form of guilt over regrets from your past. It can be dissatisfaction and restlessness, or it can be a habit, either good or bad.

Anything that enters your life and tries to get your focus off your relationship with God in the now is the "third person" who tries to rob you of your destiny, putting you into a tailspin and a very unsettled state of mind. One of satan's goals is to keep you unsettled so you will never be content with today. He does this by distracting you with thoughts of yesterday (guilt, perhaps) or tomorrow (fear of the future).

If we live in the yesterdays or the tomorrows of our lives, we cannot hear God speaking to us today.

It is important to know the difference between the leading of the Lord and the distractions that try to pull you away from Him. We need to know the difference between the voice of God and the other "voices" that compete for our time and attention.

Henry Drummond writes, "When God speaks He speaks so loudly that all the voices of the world seem dumb. And yet when God speaks He speaks so softly that no one hears the whisper but yourself."

Let His "whisper" drown out all the noisy distractions of the world.

## Leave the Nest

Most people have built comfort zones around their lives. Our comfort zones are like nests in which we feel safe and secure.

To maintain our "nests," we must design our own belief systems and value systems. The goal is to keep ourselves as comfortable as possible without ever being troubled by anything that may seem to contradict what we think, believe, or feel.

In many ways our "nests" become like impenetrable fortresses with walls so strong that they keep out anything that doesn't seem to fit with all those things that make us feel safe and comfortable.

People are afraid of the unknown. We're fearful of leaving the nest to venture into territory that is unfamiliar to us.

This may result in us rejecting a spiritual truth, something that the Holy Spirit is saying to us, we had not considered before. When we hear something different than we accustomed, we say, "No, that's not what I believe. My church doesn't teach that."

The effect of such a response is spiritual paralysis that prevents us from moving ahead in God. A religious "no" to God is as paralyzing as any other kind of no, maybe even worse, because through it we allow someone else's shadow (theology) to take command of our path and our life. Most religious systems define "following Jesus" as adhering to the doctrines of their particular denomination. But God does and will speak to us and pull us outside of the box of our accepted belief systems when they interfere with how things really are. The substance does not submit to the shadow. The shadow must respond to the substance.

The children of Israel were like that. They experienced miracles on a daily basis, and yet they did not say "yes" to God and all that He was showing them. Their food and water were supplied miraculously to them. They had a canopy of shade to keep them cool by day and a pillar of fire to keep them warm and guide them by night. Their clothing and shoes never wore out.

Their 40 years of wandering in the wilderness shows us that living in the miraculous does not necessarily entail living in the will of God, for the Israelites disobeyed Him and turned away from Him time and time again. They were still His beloved children, however, and so are we. Nonetheless, we will never experience the fullness of His plan for us until we begin to agree with Him every day, even when it violates our most sacred traditions.

In the same way that a loving parent takes care of his or her children whether they are behaving well or not, God, in His steadfast love, continued to watch over His children, as He still does today.

To step into the destiny of God, however, we must leave the "nest" behind. We must take the leap of faith and jump out of the "nest," no longer dependent on the cherished ways of the past.

Our comfort zones actually become more than distractions to us they resist the very will of God for our lives. They are like steel traps, because we don't want to hear what we don't want to hear. Many times, we don't want to hear the things that will cause us to change our lives even when it is God who is speaking them.

## Entering the Promised Land

The children of Israel grumbled instead of listening to God. Though they lived in the miraculous, they had not entered the rest of God. Their stubbornness, lack of faith, disobedience, and hardness of heart prevented them from enjoying His peace and rest. (See Hebrews 4.)

So, they had a big problem. They enjoyed the blessings God gave to them, but they wanted still more. However, they did not want the unknown, because it was fearful to them.

They must have wondered what would happen to them if they went into the Promised Land. They had been told that it was full of giants. In the Promised Land they would have to face their fears. It seemed easier to stay in the wilderness even though it had its hardships, but they were familiar with those hardships.

To enter the Promised Land they had to cross the river; otherwise, they would be stuck where they were. It's the same with you and me.

When you leave your comfort zone behind, you will cross the River Jordan. In your heart of hearts, by yielding to the Lord, you soon realize that something is beginning to change. In fact, you begin to realize that everything is changing! A wonderful sense of rest and contentment comes to you and you are able to say, "I am in the hand of the Lord, and He can do with me whatever He wants to do. He can take me wherever He wants to take me. I am content in Him."

This is the beginning of your destiny. From that point on each day becomes a new opportunity, an exciting adventure, a thrilling prospect, and a glorious experience in God.

Our journey of unfolding destiny happens within us—in the secret place of our innermost being—the deep place of the spirit where you meet with God, your heavenly Father.

God is calling you. Listen for His voice.

Jesus said, *"You did not choose Me, but I chose you and appointed you that you should go and bear fruit, and that your fruit should remain, that whatever you ask the Father in My name He may give you"* (John 15:16).

## *An Exciting Relationship*

Do you remember when you first came to know the Lord Jesus Christ? I think all of us have fond recollections of that time when everything seemed fresh, exciting, and new.

I remember those first few months after I discovered how much Jesus loved me. I *knew* Jesus loved me, and it was incredible to contemplate as well as experience His love daily. No religious restraints or distractions had been imposed upon me—yet.

I prayed, and God answered. Miracles happened on an almost daily basis. I was walking in love and newness of life. It was truly glorious.

No hard-and-fast religious rules and regulations had been shackled to my ankles—yet. I wasn't pulling a "religious ball and chain" behind me—yet.

I felt free and truly believed I could do anything through Christ. This went on for many months and years until a few things happened that challenged my faith.

Let me give you an example of the kind of thing I mean. In the early days of Destiny Image, we wanted to get our titles into a chain of major department stores for obvious reasons. Every time we tried to do so, however, the door was slammed shut in our faces!

No one in the large retail sales business seemed to even want to talk with me. They didn't seem at all interested in carrying our books. Therefore, I hired representatives to see if they could get our products in their stores, but that didn't work either.

Then, a few years ago, my son Donald walked into my office and asked, "Dad, why aren't we selling books through those department stores?"

"Well, why do you ask?"

He said, "I can't get it out of my mind. We need to get our books into those stores."

My son, in his fresh sense of excitement, had confronted me with a choice. I could have responded by saying, "That'll never happen. You have no idea how many times I've tried, only to be humiliated as they laughed me out of their offices."

Had I done so, I would have discouraged him and built walls of limitation around him. Such negative words would have started a wrong mind-set within him, causing him, in all likelihood, to envision a small company with limited prospects.

Instead, I said, "Well, what do you want to do?"

"I want to call them," he responded, "and I want to make an appointment to go see them."

"Go ahead and do it," I said. "Go for it!"

As he turned to walk out of my office, he said, "Will you go with me?"

"Yes, I will," I said.

And that's what we did, and the rest is history, for our books are now in that chain all over the world.

We can limit God, or we can walk with the God who has no limits. We can pass our limitations on to those around us, or we can encourage freshness and new ideas, keeping our past, bad experiences to ourselves. In this context, we can pass our religious restrictions on, or we can allow those around us to explore and find new possibilities that we never allowed to empower us.

The Scriptures tell us that God's mercies are new every morning. This principle is wondrous indeed. It tells us that there is nothing that needs to carry over into the next day, the next hour, the next minute, or even the next generation. The future is as pure as we allow it to be. The hearts of the innocent are as free and full of imagination and possibilities as we permit them to be. It is a shame that we seem to have the need to pass our limitations, failures, hurts, fears, and everything else negative onto the next generation—a generation that so desperately needs to know that they can do all things through Christ Jesus. Then, we could get out of the way so they *can* do all things. These are the folks who will, without question, fulfill their destiny, living each day according to the dream God has dreamed for them.

In my book, *Breaking Generational Curses*, I deal with this topic more completely.

## Never an Aimless Minute

Why were you born? What is God's magnificent purpose for your life? To state the answer to this question simply, it's to get you to the point where you will agree with Him.

George McDonald writes, "The purposes of God point to one simple end—that we should be as He is, think the same thoughts, mean the same things, possess the same blessedness." This is possible when you respond to God by yielding your life completely to Him.

To do this, you must see yourself as you really are and see God as He really is. C.S. Lewis, after a lifetime of atheism, explained his own conversion this way: "I gave in, and admitted that God was God." The dream God had for Lewis began to be fulfilled at that precise moment, and, as you know, his Christ-centered books continue to be on the best-seller lists more than fifty years after he said "yes" to Jesus. Movies inspired by these books have brought a new generation to the knowledge of Christ.

The Holy Spirit holds your destiny in His hands. Remember, He knew you before you were even born. Writing down the words God gave to him, Jeremiah proclaimed, *"Before I formed you in the womb I knew you; before you were born I sanctified you; I ordained you a prophet to the nations"* (Jer. 1:5).

Though God spoke these words personally to the prophet, they apply to each of us, as well, for it is a spiritual principle that God knew us all before we were born, forming us according to the dream He dreamed for us.

God still knows you, and all that you have gone through or are going through is designed to get you to the point where you will simply yield to His will.

You may think you're wandering aimlessly, as the ancient Israelites did, but there is never an aimless moment in your life, because God has a plan and a purpose. He is working His purpose out in your life at all times, both in the good times and the bad. He never gives up on you. Sometimes it may seem you are going in precisely the opposite direction you want to go. But when you trust Him, you know you are heading in that direction for a reason.

Paul writes, *"And we know that all things work together for good to those who love God, to those who are the called according to His purpose"* (Rom. 8:28). You have been called to fulfill God's purpose for your life, and everything that has happened to you, is happening to you, will happen to you will all work together for good in your life.

Along the way you may wander, chasing a dream that is not in God's heart for you. You may get sidetracked, and you will certainly make mistakes, but through it all you will learn, grow, and change. God is always in the process of conforming you to the image of His Son, who, like you, had to learn obedience through the things He suffered. (See Hebrews 5:8.)

But this is the point. You may be wandering because of your own rebellion. You may also be wandering because God has something for you to learn, so He needs to take you in a different direction for a season. The issue is really tied up in where you are spiritually and emotionally. If you are trusting God, you are exactly where God wants you to be. It is really that simple. We waste years trying to prove that we have found the best plans for our lives. In fact, all we are doing is burning the years away, while our destiny is held in Heaven, waiting for us to finally give up and go His way instead or our own. The more we go our own way, the more time we waste.

My sons used to dread the first three-four months of the winter school semester (January-April), because it was so intense and had very few breaks. It was always just too long and too boring.

They just didn't see the "big picture." They didn't yet understand the purpose of their education, or where it was leading them. To them, it was an aimless journey without an end or a reward.

The same is true with regard to our spiritual destiny. When God is leading us, He wants us to learn some very important lessons along the way.

The points of destiny you reach are opportunities for you to yield your life to Him. There are times during the journey when a lot of things will not be clear to you. At those times you need to trust *"...in the Lord with all your heart, and lean not on your own understanding; in all your ways acknowledge Him, and He shall direct your paths"* (Prov. 3:5-6).

I conclude this chapter with the inspiring words of Martin Luther King: "I still believe that standing up for the truth of God is the greatest thing in the world. This is the end [purpose] of life. The end of life is not to be happy. The end of life is not to achieve pleasure and avoid pain. The end of life is to do the will of God, come what may."

The focal point of your destiny, then, is to hear God's voice and agree with Him by doing His will at all times. It is then that your purpose will be fulfilled, and you will know beyond all doubt that your life *"...is hidden with Christ in God"* (Col. 3:3).

## SCRIPTURE REFERENCES FOR FURTHER STUDY

| | |
|---|---|
| Hebrews 5:8 | Matthew 6:33 |
| Colossians 3:3 | 1 John 3:2-3 |
| Proverbs 3:5-6 | James 4:8 |
| Jeremiah 1:5 | Psalm 46:10 |
| Hebrews 4 | Romans 8:28 |

Jesus said, *"My sheep hear My voice, and I know them, and they follow Me"* (John 10:27).

# CHAPTER ELEVEN

# Hearing God's Voice
## In the Now

If you don't recognize the voice of the Lord, it is time you learn how. God knows He wants to talk to you. He has so many exciting and wonderful things to say to you. But some people think they're not "good enough" to hear the voice of the Lord or that they haven't lived the "right kind of life" that would enable them to do so. Some may even think that being able to hear the Lord's voice is a special ability that's reserved for only a select few.

The Lord Jesus, however, is clear when He says, *"My sheep hear My voice."* If you name the Name of Jesus, then you are one of His sheep and it is your right and awesome privilege to hear His voice. It is available, powerful, and necessary.

We need to break through our walls of resistance, to climb out of our "nests," to leave our comfort zones, and listen carefully to Him.

As we mentioned in the preceding chapter, the points of destiny we reach in our lives are opportunities to agree with God, to hear His voice, to do His will.

To do this, as we also mentioned before, we must leave the nest (our place of comfort) behind. A nest is where a baby bird's needs are completely supplied. Think of a family of eagles, for example. The eaglets don't want to leave their cozy, comfortable, and warm nest. Knowing this would be true, their parents built the nest in such a way that its bottom is layered with thorns and thistles.

They put a bed of soft feathers and grass on top. This makes a soft cushion for their eaglets. When the eaglets get so big that they begin to fight each other for room in the nest, however, the parents begin removing the top, soft layer so that their offspring will no longer be so comfortable. In fact, their bodies will be pricked and pierced by the thistles and thorns as they engage in "sibling rivalry," causing them to want to leave the nest altogether.

The parent eagles do this because they know it's best for their offspring. They want their eaglets to experience life outside of the nest. In the same way, God will sometimes remove the soft "down" from our nests. He does this because He loves us.

I have often wondered what would have happened if I had said "no" the first time I received an invitation to minister in Italy. At the time I was struggling physically. Though Cathy went with me and was a huge help to me, it was almost as if I needed a third person to go along just to take care of me.

It would have been so much easier to stay at home in my soft and cozy "nest." But God had other plans for me, and I'm so glad I did not miss out on His purposes for my life and the lives of the wonderful people of Italy.

Incredible things are happening there because of God's faithfulness to His people. For example, Pastor Peter Evangelista, who now is founding publisher of Destiny Image Europe, has been invited to speak in conferences all over Europe, and the Pentecostal churches there are experiencing new growth and freshness.

## Carpe Diem!

Few of us really know how to "seize the day," to capture the present moment, and to live in it fully, but this is what Jesus wants for each of us. This is the meaning of the Latin phrase, *Carpe Diem.*

Many Christians are unwilling to live in the now. It's as if they would rather spend their time worrying about what happened yesterday or hoping for something to happen tomorrow. They may say things like, "Jesus is coming tomorrow;" "I'm going to get healed tomorrow;" "My kids are going to get better tomorrow," or "A wonderful blessing is going to happen tomorrow." It's always tomorrow, but never today. But Jesus lives neither in tomorrow or yesterday for that matter. He lives in today, the now of life.

It's so pointless to spend most of your time lamenting over what went on before or worrying about what might happen in the future. As someone has said, "Worry is like a rocking chair. It gives you something to do, but it doesn't take you anywhere." How true. Most of the things we worry about never materialize! The real hope for our worry is not the rocking chair, it is trusting in our God who is the God of the now.

We may hope that things will get better tomorrow or sometime in the future. Hope is certainly a good thing, but experiencing the fullness of life in the here-and-now is far more rewarding than just hoping ever could be.

Our God is the great I AM. He is the One who supersedes the restrictions of time. He is totally alive in the present tense. To Him, the future is now. To Him, eternity is now. It's the present moments of your life that count to Him.

His Word declares, *"Today, if you will hear His voice, do not harden your hearts as in the rebellion"* (Heb. 3:15).

He wants you to hear His voice today. To experience His life and His Presence today. To know His lovingkindness today.

This is the day the Lord has made, and He wants you to rejoice and be glad in it. (See Psalm 118:24.)

Let the attitudes of your heart reflect this truth each day.

Here is a good way to start your day: "This is the day the Lord has made. This is the day of rejoicing. I will be glad today. This day is going to be a wonderful day, full of the blessings of the Lord. I'm going to hear the Lord's voice today. I'm going to do what He wants me to do today."

## *Are You Satisfied?*

The Bible tells us that godliness with contentment is great gain for us. (See First Timothy 6:6.) This verse is describing a rich and full sense of satisfaction that absolutely nothing in the world can ever provide for us.

Too often, though, we may feel unsatisfied—unsatisfied with our kids, our jobs, our churches, our homes, our automobiles, our finances, our calling, our spouses, our neighbors, and so many other things. We may feel restless and unfulfilled, and we want things to change.

This is natural, but it's so much better to wake up each morning and say, "Yes, Lord, I'm satisfied. I'm satisfied with You and all You've provided for me. I'm going to live this day for You."

Many people, even some Christians, will say, "I'm trying to find myself." I know one person who told me he was having problems in his life, so he decided to go to a South Pacific island "to find himself." He spent three months there, searching for his own personal identity.

Being on a South Pacific island for three months wouldn't be too bad, but I doubt if he truly "found himself" there! He had forgotten that the perfect key for finding himself is not a trip to an isolated island, but it is in losing oneself. Jesus said, *"And he who does not take his cross and follow after Me is not worthy of Me. He who finds his life will lose it, and he who loses his life for My sake will find it"* (Matt. 10:38-39).

170

We need to open our hearts to the Lord today. We need to break through any hardness of heart—the calluses that come from the hurts and hardships of life—and find our true identity in the Lord.

## *The Courage to Say "Yes"*

It takes courage to say "yes" to God. It takes courage to listen for His voice and follow Him.

We need to know Him as the ever-present I Am. The "something better" we hope for has already come. His Name is Jesus. Eternity has already begun.

One man who had a wonderful job came to me for counsel. He said, "I am not satisfied. I'm waiting to serve the Lord. There must be something more for me. I'm waiting to hear God tell me how He wants me to serve Him."

I just didn't get it. I couldn't understand what he was after. As we prayed together and sought the Lord together, God revealed something to him that He had already revealed to me. He showed this man that He had put him where he was, that he was to be content in his present circumstances, no matter how long. I was so glad this man could hear this from the Lord! It was an 'out of the nest' word from the Lord and it changed his life. Had I shared that with him, he probably would not have responded so well! Thank God for the Holy Spirit who speaks to hearts even when we may not want to hear what God is saying!

This was a true revelation to him, and it resulted in a sense of peace, satisfaction, and contentment that the man had not experienced for a long time. Though it took courage for him to agree with God on this, the man finally said, "Yes, Lord."

Sometimes it takes more courage to say "yes" to God in the present circumstances of your life than it might take to head out for the mission field or embark on some kind of traveling ministry. The daily grind of life and the nitty-gritty details of every day life may seem monotonous and burdensome, but God speaks to us there—in the here-and-now of our daily existence.

In *My Utmost for His Highest,* Oswald Chambers writes, "It is the dull, bald, dreary, commonplace day, with commonplace duties and people, that kills the burning heart unless we have learned the secret of abiding in Jesus." He's exactly right—we must live, move, and have our being in the Lord every day, experiencing His Manifest Presence no matter where we are or what we are doing. But there is another step! It is among the dull, boring and monotonous that He wants to show His glory. It is often dull and boring because we are not listening to or maybe not obeying the voice of the Lord. His Presence excites and enlightens the most tiresome of lives!!

Abiding in Jesus is actually resting in Him and in His perfect will. This is what gives us the courage to say, "Yes, Lord. I love you now. I will live for you where I am. I'm content with all you've provided for me. I'm satisfied with my job. I will love my spouse more than ever. I will enjoy my children now. I will walk in the joy of the Lord throughout this day. I am open to you. Speak to me lead me, guide me so I can fulfill the your dream for right here, right now."

This approach to daily living changes everything, for you're no longer waiting to serve Him; you're serving Him now. You're not waiting for something great to happen, because you know something great is always happening. You're not waiting to hear His voice, for you know He is always speaking to you.

If you hear His voice, He will lead you each step of the way. This will give you the courage to follow Him wherever He leads you.

## *The Joy of the Lord Is Your Strength*

The happiest and most powerful believer is the one who has learned to say "yes" to God in the here-and-now of life. This person's heart is open to all God has for him. Instead of hardening his heart, this believer listens for the voice of God.

Too often Christians may think, "If I say 'yes' to God and hear His voice, He'll say, 'Go to Africa' or something like that." The more likely scenario, however, is that God would say something in the here-and-now, such as, *"Bake a cake for your neighbor"* or *"Make spaghetti for your husband"* or *"Play with the children on the floor"* or *"Stay home with your family."*

The fleshy response to such ideas might be, "But that's not exciting. I want to do something that's great and life-changing for You, Lord."

When we aren't living in the Presence of God in the now, we don't understand that the things with eternal value are the things we do for others. It may seem like a cliché, but it's nonetheless true that "Only one life will soon be past; only what's done for Christ will last."

For example, the time and training we invest into the lives of our children will last for all eternity. What could be more important than spending time with them? What is more important than loving our spouse? What is more important than doing something for our neighbors? These are all extremely important things to do, and the beauty in this approach is that they can be done in the here-and-now.

When we don't live in the now, we don't realize that, as parents, we are raising mighty warriors in God's kingdom. We are teaching these little "men and women of God" things that will become part of their lives forever.

There is great joy to be found in doing what God wants you to do in the present moments and the "todays" of your life. No joy can compare with the joy you receive from agreeing with God's will for you and doing what He wants you to do.

The ancient prophet Nehemiah knew how to say "yes" to God in the present moments of his life, and this is what enabled him to declare, *"...for this day is holy to our Lord. Do not sorrow, for the joy of the Lord is your strength"* (Neh. 8:10). This day—today—

is holy to the Lord. It is the day He has made for you. Rejoice and be glad in it. The joy you will derive from doing so will bring great joy to your heart and life.

## Little Things Can Be Great Things

In God's Kingdom little things often become great things. Not long after Cathy and I were married, we lived in a fourth-floor apartment on Fort Street, in Shippensburg, Pennsylvania. The apartment was so small that I would almost put my hand through the ceiling when I tried to put on my shirt each morning! Once, I even broke a light bulb while doing so.

We were both working full-time and attending university there. I was also the leader of a campus Christian group with a membership of 125. I had been walking with the Lord for two months, longer than most of the others, so they made me their "leader"!

The job I took was in the campus snack bar. My hope was to be the cashier or someone who did stock inventory or a cook, but those things were not meant to be. Instead, my job was cleaning the bathrooms, scrubbing the floors, and clearing the tables. It was unpleasant work that sometimes even involved cleaning up "stuff" left behind by drunken college students.

Take my word for it, it definitely was not a glamorous job! I began to moan about it, always wondering why I had to do such awful tasks. Why do I have to clean bathrooms and scrub floors, I would ask. As I washed the commodes in the restrooms, I would say to God, "Lord, you can't mean for me to do this stuff!"

Meanwhile, Cathy had the job of cooking in the snack bar, and I must admit, a little jealousy crept into my heart!

I would work all afternoon. The meeting of our Christian group took place at 6:30 in the evening. This meant that I had to take a complete change of clothes to work with me and take a shower before the meeting.

While scrubbing a toilet one day, God spoke to me. He said, *"You are not cleaning that toilet for anybody else but Me. They didn't tell you to clean it; I did!"*

In that nitty-gritty, down-and-dirty moment God spoke to me. I heard His voice in the now of my existence. I was on my knees scrubbing the commode when He spoke so clearly to me, and it was a life-changing moment for me.

Truly, it was a living revelation of this Bible truth: *"And whatever you do, do it heartily, as to the Lord and not to men, knowing that from the Lord you will receive the reward of the inheritance; for you serve the Lord Christ"* (Col. 3:23-24).

With renewed joy and a definite sense of purpose, I got up, went over and picked up a bucket of steaming water, mixed cleaning chemicals into it, put my gloves and mask on, got back on my knees, and began to scrub! I scrubbed as I had never scrubbed before!

The result was sparkling toilets, clean sinks, and an immaculate floor as well as a whole new attitude, a freshness of spirit, and a deep and abiding sense of accomplishment and joy. I was cleaning commodes for Jesus now, and I was determined they would be cleaner than ever before!

Word of my good work began to spread, and some of the ladies would wait to use the bathroom each day till they knew I had completed my cleaning job. A line actually formed outside the bathroom as I was cleaning them! Seems that working for Jesus paid benefits to those around me as well. Hm, I bet there is a book in that statement....

I'm sure there were times when I smelled like cleaning fluid and Lysol as I prayed for people in our meeting, but that was okay, because I knew I was doing what God wanted me to do.

I learned then that it is always important to say "yes" to the Father, for this is the prayer He loves to answer. I learned that it's necessary to agree with Him so that His dream for me will be fulfilled. I understood that His plan will not automatically come to pass in my life. I must permit it by submitting my will to His will. I learned that it is vital to hear His voice in the here-and-now.

I could have been stubborn and hard-hearted and resisted His will, but He gave me His grace that enabled me to say, "Yes, Lord."

In *God's Will: Our Dwelling Place*, Andrew Murray writes:

And then, there is God's will in His eternal, worldwide purpose. The vision of the will that embraces all creation has made me part of it. It has made His own glory dependent on its and my own destiny. It enlarges my heart to feel that my true and only glory is to yield myself as a willing instrument to its service, and to live only so that His will may triumph throughout the whole earth.

There is nothing on this planet more exciting to know than this: In the midst of all the grand things God has purposed for this earth, He remembered me. In His remembrance, He dreamed me right in the middle of it. He intends for me to play a part in the unfolding of His master dream for all generations and for all time.

***"TODAY IF YOU HEAR HIS VOICE, DO NOT HARDEN YOUR HEARTS..."*** **(Hebrews 3:15).**

## SCRIPTURE REFERENCES FOR FURTHER STUDY

| | |
|---|---|
| Deuteronomy 6:4 | Colossians 3:23-24 |
| Romans 10:14 | Nehemiah 8:10 |
| John 16:13 | Matthew 10:38-39 |
| 1 Corinthians 2:9 | 1 Timothy 6:6 |
| Galatians 3:2 | John 10:27 |
| Isaiah 40:21 | John 10:3 |

# REFLECTIONS

# REFLECTIONS

# REFLECTIONS

# REFLECTIONS

# REFLECTIONS

# REFLECTIONS

# REFLECTIONS

# REFLECTIONS

# Contact Information

## DON NORI

**c/o Destiny Image Publishers**
167 Walnut Bottom Rd.
Shippensburg, PA 17257

**Ph: 717-532-3040        Ext: 124**

**E-mail: dfn@destinyimage.com**

---

*To understand where you are
going, first you must know
where you have been.*

## SECRETS OF THE
## MOST HOLY PLACE VOL. 1
### BY DON NORI

Here is a prophetic parable you will read again and again. The winds of God are blowing, drawing you to His Life within the Veil of the Most Holy Place. There you begin to see as you experience a depth of relationship your heart has yearned for. This book is a living, dynamic experience with God.

ISBN 1-56043-076-1

The sins of our fathers do not have to torment us. Our sins do not have to chase after our children.

## BREAKING GENERATIONAL CURSES
### BY DON NORI

This is a serious book that has real serious answers for all of us. It is a practical guide for hope and healing in our lives and in all the lives we touch. These answers are not spooky or mystical. They are practical and predictable.

Each generation's sin should be locked in that generation. This book tells you why and also tells you how to be certain they stay in that generation.

ISBN 0-914903-48-9

Heaven is my destination, but it is not my destiny. Many will reach their destination, but few will achieve their destiny.

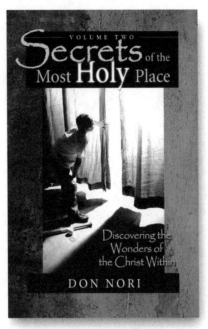

## SECRETS OF THE MOST HOLY PLACE VOL. 2
## BY DON NORI

Prophetic parable matures into prophetic reality as His presence draws us into the realm of "all God." Here, what we believe becomes what we experience and what we know becomes flesh in mere mortal man.

This book is not for the casual reader. It is for those who hunger, not for education, but for reality; not for religion, but for Him.

ISBN 0-7684-2175-6

The first steps to a life within the
Most Holy Place must be taken
into His Manifest Presence.

## HIS MANIFEST PRESENCE
## BY DON NORI

We must move from David's Tabernacle worship to Solomon's
Temple, where *His Manifest Presence* is experienced, if we
are to live His fullness and His protection through the tumul-
tuous days ahead. Here are some ways in which you can enter
His presence.

ISBN 0-914903-48-9

# The secret to knowing God's plans and desires for your personal destiny!

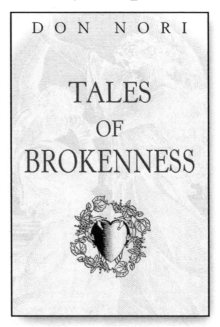

## TALES OF BROKENNESS
## BY DON NORI

Brokenness—the disdain of tyrants and the wonder of kings. Her mystery has eluded the intellectual and empowered the noble of heart. From her bosom flows the power and compassion to change the world.

In *Tales of Brokenness* you'll meet this companion who never forgets her need of mercy, never forgets the grace that flows on her behalf. She is the secret to knowing God's plans and desires and to finding your way to your personal destiny.

ISBN 0-7684-2074-1

# A story of True Love...
# and the fulfillment it brings!

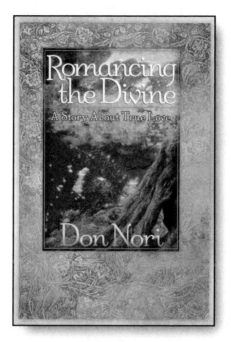

## ROMANCING THE DIVINE
## BY DON NORI

*Romancing the Divine* is a tale of every person's journey to find the reality of God. It is a tale of hope, a search for eternal love, and for all the possibilities we have always imagined would be the conclusion of such a search. In this story you will most assuredly recognize your own search for God, and discover the divine fulfillment that His love brings.

ISBN 0-7684-2053-9

Additional copies of this book and other
book titles from DESTINY IMAGE are
available at your local bookstore.

Call toll free: 1-800-722-6774.

Send a request for a catalog to:

## Destiny Image® Publishers, Inc.

P.O. Box 310
Shippensburg, PA 17257-0310

*"Speaking to the Purposes of God for this*
*Generation and for the Generations to Come."*

## For a complete list of our titles,
## visit us at www.destinyimage.com